A Slice of Life

Documents of Practice Series

General Editor

Joel T. Rosenthal
State University of New York at Stony Brook

A Slice of Life

Selected Documents of Medieval English Peasant Experience

Edited, Translated, and
with an Introduction
by
Edwin Brezette DeWindt

Published for TEAMS
(The Consortium for the Teaching of the Middle Ages)

by

Medieval Institute Publications

WESTERN MICHIGAN UNIVERSITY

Kalamazoo, Michigan—1996

© 1996 by the Board of the Medieval Institute

Second Printing 2001
Third Printing 2005

Printed in the United States of America

Cover design by Linda K. Judy

ISBN 1-879288-73-7

Library of Congress Cataloging-in-Publication Data

A slice of life : selected documents of medieval English peasant
experience / edited, translated, and with an introduction by Edwin
Brezette DeWindt.
    p. cm.
    Includes bibliographical references (p.).
    ISBN 1-879288-73-7 (pbk. : alk. paper)
    1. Peasantry--England--Warboys--History--Sources. 2. Land tenure-
-England--Warboys--History--Sources. 3. Court records--England-
-Warboys. 4. Middle Ages. I. DeWindt, Edwin Brezette.
    II. Consortium for the Teaching of the Middle Ages.
    HD1339.G7S48   1996   96-45726
    942.6'5403--dc20   CIP

Contents

Acknowledgements

This small collection of documents is designed to be used by undergraduates interested in exploring the kinds of texts historians use to construct a picture of medieval English peasant life. It came into being at the suggestion of Professor Joel T. Rosenthal of the State University of New York at Stony Brook. In the course of putting this collection together, I have received the kind and generous cooperation of the staffs of the British Library and the Public Record Office, London. Closer to home, I thank my colleagues in the History Department at the University of Detroit Mercy for their enthusiasm for the project, especially Dr. Sarah Stever Gravelle, Chair of the Department of History, Dr. Gregory Sumner, Dr. Thomas Brown, Kathleen Bush, Assistant Dean of the College of Liberal Arts, and Dr. Catherine Caraher, former Assistant Dean and Chair of the Department of History. I am also grateful to those students who, over the years, have made our joint, albeit brief, classroom sojourns into the social history of the medieval English village exciting and rewarding, especially Moira Kordel, Anne Dwyer, Laura Masetti, Theresa Darwish, Nancy Hayes, and Joan Miranda. Finally, I thank my wife, Anne Reiber DeWindt, who makes this all possible.

Introduction

The Medieval English Peasantry

An old commonplace states that medieval society was divided into those who worked, those who fought, and those who prayed.[1] Whether or not this ever was an accurate description of reality, it is certainly true that in England during the Middle Ages those who worked overwhelmingly outnumbered those who fought and those who prayed combined! The medieval English world, like that of continental Europe during the same time period, was not an urban world, a world made up primarily of cities and towns. Rather, it was a world rooted in agriculture, characterized by a wide variety of human settlements and communities, from isolated farmsteads to scattered hamlets and nucleated villages,[2] and inhabited by men

---

1. The most comprehensive study of the concept is Georges Duby, *The Three Orders: Feudal Society Imagined*, tr. Arthur Goldhammer, with a forward by Thomas N. Bisson (Chicago, 1980).

2. The origins of such forms of rural living arrangements are the subject of heated debate among historians and archaeologists. Even their antiquity is not taken for granted. Was the nucleated village, for example, an old and almost natural product of human needs to combine labor and resources so as to engage in more effective and efficient types of agriculture, or was it a more recent (i.e., eleventh–twelfth century) creation imposed upon rural cultivators from above by feudal lords eager to consolidate their resources and power? At the present stage of inquiry, we simply do not know the answer to that question. Evidence can be found to support either position—and a broad spectrum of other positions in between. Most likely, when all is said and done, there will be no one answer at all. This is admittedly a sloppy and untidy state of affairs for knowledge to be in, but, after all, human life itself

1

Introduction

and women whom scholars have usually described as "peasants."[3] Some historians have assumed that approximately 90
percent of the medieval population consisted of these rural

---

is sloppy and untidy. That is what makes it challenging and exciting, and that
is what makes the various attempts to understand and make sense out of it
equally exciting, stimulating, and, even, exhilarating. See Brian K. Roberts
and R. E. Glasscock, eds., *Villages, Fields and Frontiers: Studies in
European Rural Settlement in the Medieval and Early Modern Periods.
Papers Presented at the Meeting of the Permanent European Conference for
the Study of the Rural Landscape* (Oxford, 1983); Michael Aston, David
Austin, and Christopher Dyer, eds., *The Rural Settlements of Medieval
England. Studies Dedicated to Maurice Beresford and John Hurst* (Oxford,
1989); Brian K. Roberts, *Rural Settlement* (London, 1987), and *The Making
of the English Village: A Study in Historical Geography* (Harlow, 1987); and
Leopold Genicot, *Rural Communities in the Medieval West* (Baltimore, 1990).

3. The word "peasant" (French: *paysan,* Italian: *paisano*) literally means
"country dweller." For a straightforward definition of the term as used by
most medieval historians, see Rodney H. Hilton, *The English Peasantry in
the Later Middle Ages. The Ford Lectures for 1973, and Related Studies*
(Oxford, 1979), esp. pp. 3–19. The word itself has recently become the
subject of some controversy concerning its appropriateness in being applied
to medieval England. The British historian and anthropologist Alan
Macfarlane, in a provocative and controversial book (*The Origins of English
Individualism: The Family, Property, and Social Transition* [Oxford, 1979])
and in subsequent publications (*Marriage and Love in England: Modes of
Reproduction, 1300–1840* [Oxford, 1986], *The Culture of Capitalism* [Oxford,
1987]) has proposed that medieval England did not have a peasant society at
all. His argument is based on descriptions of traditional peasant societies
produced by anthropologists and especially draws upon work done on the
Polish peasantry in the nineteenth century. One could agree, of course, that
there were certainly not any nineteenth-century Polish peasants in thirteenth-
century England, but that would be trivializing what is, in fact, a set of
observations that forces historians to consider the broad social variety within
rural society throughout the Western world. Therefore, whether we choose to
call these rural cultivators "peasants," "farmers," or even "bumpkins," it is
important to realize that the term is only a label of convenience and does not
carry with it an iron-clad set of definitions.

Introduction

cultivators,[4] and, even given the notorious problems associated with trying to arrive at meaningful figures about medieval population,[5] it is probably a reasonable assumption.

Peasants, then, were everywhere, yet we know less about them—both singly and collectively—than we think we know about knights, bishops, monks, merchants, noble ladies, barons, and kings. The reasons for this are many, and none of them is sinister. Basically, it is a matter of source material. Put quite simply: medieval peasants did not write.[6] As a result, information about them is to be found in a disparate body of sources. Literary sources are especially well known by the

---

4. See J. Ambrose Raftis, *Tenure and Mobility: Studies in the Social History of the Mediaeval English Village* (Toronto, 1964) [hereafter cited *Tenure and Mobility*]. Also, see idem, "Peasant Mobility and Freedom in Medieval England," *Report of the Canadian Historical Association* (1965), p. 120.

5. For discussion of medieval English population and the problems involved in obtaining meaningful and reliable demographic figures, see Josiah Cox Russell, *British Medieval Population* (Albuquerque, 1948), and the same author's *Medieval Demography: Essays, with a preface by David Herlihy* (New York, 1987). See also E. A. Wrigley and R. S. Schofield, *The Population History of England, 1541–1871: A Reconstruction* (Cambridge, 1981).

6. This is the kind of statement historians try to avoid at all cost, since there is always the possibility—however remote and unlikely it may be—that someday someone will stumble upon a document in some archive somewhere that is, in fact, the diary or memoirs or record-book of a medieval peasant. That some medieval English peasants were, in fact, able to read and even write is a fact. In the small market town of Ramsey, for example, located in what were once the Huntingdonshire fens (since drained and turned into a landscape strangely reminiscent of northern Ohio), the court rolls contain examples of both skills. In 1321, letters were stolen from a house, while the first court roll of 1591 includes the actual signatures of several of the court jurors. See Edwin B. DeWindt, ed., *The Court Rolls of Ramsey, Hepmangrove and Bury, 1268–1600* (Toronto, 1990), nos. 1321:9 and 1590 [1], n. 17.

Introduction

general public, and Langland, Chaucer, the Pearl Poet, Gower, et al., and ballads have all been plundered for glimpses of peasant life. The other major body of written material is less well known—a vast number of records, both private and public, embracing seignorial account rolls,[7] cartularies,[8] rentals,[9] private charters,[10] royal court records,[11] national

7. Account rolls are annual reports by the reeve or bailiff of a manor to the lord of all receipts and expenses for the manor. An example of an account roll is translated in this volume (*infra*, pp. 76–88). For discussion of account rolls, see *infra*, pp. 33–36.

8. Cartularies were collections made by landlords of records considered valuable for estate administration. They can contain almost anything—whatever the lord, or his agents, felt was worth keeping. Thus, a cartulary could include *extents* (detailed lists of manorial properties, labor obligations, rents, dues and services, even the names of tenants), court cases, charters, inventories of manorial stock or even of personal furnishings. A useful guide to such records, as well as to edited and published account rolls, rentals, etc., is E. C. Mullins, *Texts and Calendars. An Analytical Guide to Serial Publications* (London, 1958); also E. C. Mullins, *Texts and Calendars II: An Analytical Guide to Serial Publications, 1957–1982* (London, 1983).

9. Rentals were lists of tenants, the properties they held, and the rent due.

10. Charters are the medieval equivalent of deeds to property. They contain details of sales, exchanges or outright grants of property between individuals or between individuals and institutions. Tens of thousands of such documents survive and are preserved in such places as the Public Record Office and the British Library in London, private collections of manuscripts, and in many local, county record offices and the record collections of other public and private institutions and corporations (e.g., Oxford and Cambridge college libraries). Useful guides to some charter collections are: H. J. Ellis and F. B. Bickley, eds., *Index to the Charters and Rolls in the Department of Manuscripts, British Museum*, 2 vols. (London, 1900, 1912); *A Descriptive Catalogue of Ancient Deeds in the Public Record Office, prepared under the superintendence of the Deputy Keeper of the Records*, 4 vols. (London, 1890 et seq.); and the various publications and reports of the Historical Manuscripts Commission.

4

surveys of estates,[12] tax rolls,[13] and local village court rolls.[14] Still another source of important information on peasant life is archaeology, which concerns itself with recovering the

---

11. The number, and variety, of surviving royal court records is staggering. Records of the royal courts are preserved beginning with the reign of Richard I (the Lion-Heart) in 1189–99. The medieval records embrace the courts of Common Pleas, King's Bench, Exchequer, Assize rolls, Eyre rolls, the proceedings of the courts of Star Chamber, Wards and Requests, Chancery, and other more specialized courts. (A convenient introduction to the range of this material is *Guide to the Contents of the Public Record Office* [London, 1965], esp. vol. 1.) Selections from these records have been edited in several volumes published by the Selden Society, while other editions of legal records can be located in Mullins' *Texts and Calendars.*

12. The most famous of such documents are the so-called Domesday Book of 1086 and the Hundred Rolls of 1274 and 1279. For discussion of the former, see Frederic William Maitland, *Domesday Book and Beyond: Three Essays in the Early History of England* (Cambridge, 1897); Christopher Holdsworth, ed., *Domesday Essays* (Exeter, 1986); for the Hundred Rolls—a sprawling inquiry by the Crown into the holdings of tenants-in-chief containing breakdowns of the latters' manors by size, number of holdings and tenants, rents and services, and other resources—see Helen M. Cam, *The Hundred and the Hundred Rolls: An Outline of Local Government in Medieval England* (London, 1930), and Evgeny Alekseevich Kosminsky, *Studies in the Agrarian History of England in the Thirteenth Century,* trans. Ruth Kisch, ed. Rodney H. Hilton (Oxford, 1956).

13. Taxes on personal movable property, called subsidies, were imposed and collected as early as the reign of Henry III and continued up to the seventeenth century. A complete guide can be found in The List and Index series published by the Public Record Office.

14. Village, or manorial, court rolls are preserved in local record offices, private collections, institutional archives, the British Library, and the Public Record Office.

physical evidence of everyday life.[15]

All these sources pose challenges to the historian. Literary works present imaginative portraits of rural men and women, but Piers the Plowman and Chaucer's miller and reeve are artistic creations by men who did not live in the countryside. The authors were Londoners—one a chantry priest, the other a government official. Their portraits are certainly lifelike, vivid, and—especially in the case of Chaucer—realistic and three-dimensional. But it would be extremely unwise to try and categorize the experiences of thousands of real men and women from figures invented by literary genius.

What historians want is the ability to get close to actual individual peasant men and women. But historians do not necessarily get what they want. It might be thought that the administrative and legal records of manors, villages, and the royal government would supply that desired closeness to the peasantry, and in some ways they do, but not without presenting difficulties of their own. First, the extents, rentals, surveys, and account rolls generated by medieval English estate administration can and do provide historians with valuable information about peasant landholding—the tenements themselves and the obligations attached to them. But such documents see peasants only as the landlords saw them, and in one

---

15. Useful introductions to archaeology, and especially medieval archaeology, are Helen Clarke, *The Archaeology of Medieval England* (London, 1984); John Steane, *The Archaeology of Medieval England and Wales* (London, 1985); Kevin Greene, *Archaeology: An Introduction: The History, Principles, and Methods of Modern Archaeology* (London, 1991); Brian Hayden, *Archaeology: The Science of Once and Future Things* (New York, 1993); Keith Branigan, *Archaeology Explained* (London, 1993); Andrew Chamberlain, *Human Remains* (London, 1994); and James Rackham, *Animal Bones* (London, 1994).

Introduction

particular context: as tenants. Villagers who were not tenants do not appear in these records. Second, such documents do not reveal the relationship of peasants to their *lands*, as opposed to their tenurial relationship to their *lords*. The range of intra- and extra-village involvement in landholding through sub-letting and participation in local and regional land markets is rarely reflected in such records.[16] Just as important, other economic activities in the *village* as opposed to the *manor* are absent from these documents. Information about such other economic activities must be found in local court rolls, royal court records, and subsidy rolls. When combined with data in accounts and extents, these records allow the historian to explore the degree and nature of local and regional markets and general marketing activity, adding further dimensions to a knowledge and understanding of peasant economy.[17]

Indeed, it is the records of courts in particular that have offered historians more detailed and varied information on

---

16. On the peasant land market in medieval England, see P. D. A. Harvey, ed., *The Peasant Land Market in Medieval England* (Oxford, 1989); C.N.L. Brooke and M.M. Postan, eds., *Carte Nativorum: A Peterborough Abbey Cartulary of the Fourteenth Century*. Publications of the Northamptonshire Record Society XX (Oxford, 1960); and Anne Reiber DeWindt, "A Peasant Land Market and its Participants," *Midland History* IV, nos. 3 and 4 (Autumn, 1978), pp. 142–59.

17. See Kathleen Biddick, "Missing Links: Taxable Wealth, Markets and Stratification among Medieval English Peasants," *Journal of Interdisciplinary History* 18 (1987), pp. 277–98. See also Kathleen Biddick, *The Other Economy: Pastoral Husbandry on a Medieval Estate* (Berkeley, 1989); James Masschaele, "Market Rights in Thirteenth-Century England," *English Historical Review* 107 (1992), pp. 78–89; David L. Farmer, "Two Wiltshire Manors and their Markets," *Agricultural History Review* 37 (1989), pp. 1–11; and David L. Farmer, "Marketing the Produce of the Countryside, 1200–1500," in Edward Miller, ed., *The Agrarian History of England and Wales, Vol. III: 1348–1500* (Cambridge, 1991), pp. 324–430.

Introduction

English peasant life than could ever be possible from a reliance on extents, rentals, and accounts alone. Common law records—the rolls of the courts of Common Pleas, King's Bench, Assizes, Gaol Deliveries, and Coroners' inquests—and related professional legal literature provide glimpses of peasants as jurors, litigants, witnesses, felons, and victims, while the cases themselves, as reported, are often detailed enough to permit substantial penetration into the realities of everyday living.[18] Especially, they show peasants involved in varying relationships with the machinery of royal justice: as individuals whose actions were supervised or monitored by the courts, who seek the courts' aid in redressing personal wrongs, or who play a role in judicial processes of criminal presentment and fact-finding.[19]

The records of non-royal courts—the so-called "village" or "manorial" courts—are even richer in the amount and variety of information they contain. The village court rolls of medieval England are not uniform in either content or form. They

---

18. This remains true even when allowances are made for the possible formulaic quality of entries, their sometime superficiality, and, ultimately, their accuracy or reliability in recording the truth. On this question, see Thomas Green, *Verdict According to Conscience: Perspectives on the English Criminal Trial Jury, 1200–1800* (Chicago, 1985). See also Michael T. Clanchy, *From Memory to Written Record : England, 1066-1307* (Oxford, 1993). For examples of the use of common law records—especially Coroners' rolls and Gaol Delivery rolls—in reconstructing aspects of peasant life, see Barbara A. Hanawalt, *The Ties That Bound: Peasant Families in Medieval England* (Oxford, 1986), and *Crime and Conflict in English Communities, 1300–1348* (Cambridge, Mass., 1979).

19. See Anne Reiber DeWindt and Edwin Brezette DeWindt, eds., *Royal Justice and the Mediaeval English Countryside,* 2 vols. (Toronto, 1981). See also Robert B. Goheen, "Peasant Politics? Village Communities and the Crown in Fifteenth-Century England," *American Historical Review* 96 (1991), pp. 42–62.

8

Introduction

were ostensibly seignorial in nature, records of the court that
the lord of a manor provided for his tenants, presided over by
his steward. At least in theory, such courts existed primarily as
a vehicle for the lord to exercise power over and extract
money—in the form of fines and amercements—from the
residents of his manor. Some historians still see them as fundamentally feudal instruments of oppression and exploitation.
Others see them as a more complex and complicated institution,
part a manifestation of lordship, part an institution reflective of
and responsive to the needs of men and women involved in
relationships—personal and familial, private and public, social
and economic—separate from, or supplementary to, manorial
associations.[20] Certainly they were multi-faceted institutions.
Some were *views of frankpledge*, or courts *leet*, wherein a
manorial lord exercised certain powers normally reserved to

---

20. On court rolls and manor/village courts, see Frederic William Maitland,
ed., *Select Pleas in Manorial and other Seignorial Courts*, Selden Society 2
(London, 1888); Frederic William Maitland and W. P. Baldon, eds., *The
Court Baron, being Precedents for use in Seignorial Courts and other Local
Courts, together with Select Pleas from the Bishop of Ely's Court at
Littleport*, Selden Society 4 (London, 1888); Warren O. Ault, *Private
Jurisdiction in England* (New Haven, 1923); Warren O. Ault, *Open-field
Farming in Medieval England: A Study of Village By-laws* (London, 1972),
and *Open-field Husbandry and the Village Community: A Study of Agrarian
By-laws in Medieval England* (Philadelphia, 1965); J. Ambrose Raftis, *Tenure
and Mobility*; Edwin Brezette DeWindt, *Land and People in Holywell-cum-
Needingworth: Structures of Tenure and Patterns of Social Organization in
an East Midlands Village, 1250–1457* (Toronto, 1972); Edward Britton, *The
Community of the Vill: A Study of the History of the Family and Village Life
in Fourteenth-century England* (Toronto, 1977); and Zvi Razi, *Life, Marriage
and Death in a Medieval Parish: Economy and Demography in Halesown,
1270–1400* (Cambridge, 1980). For a contemporary legal historian who views
the manor court as especially a vehicle for lords to impose their wills on their
dependent and reluctant peasants, see John S. Beckerman, "Procedural
Innovation and Institutional Change in Medieval English Manorial Courts,"
Law and History Review 10 (1992), pp. 197–252.

Introduction

sheriffs[21] and supervised compliance with national standards on brewing and baking and exacted monetary penalties for lesser criminal or disruptive behavior by the residents of the manor. Other courts were known as *courts baron*, or "honor" courts, wherein lords exercised jurisdiction over their major tenants and oversaw their tenurial inter-relationships with each other. Yet another type was the simple *curia*, or "court"—a meeting of the local inhabitants to enforce agricultural obligations, regulate the use of common, gleaning privileges, and correct disruptions to, or interferences with, roads, ditches, streams, as well as conduct miscellaneous business including regulation of obnoxious pets and annoying farm animals. In reality, it was not unusual for a single court to embrace all these activities simultaneously, or in distinctive combinations.[22]

---

21. In the so-called "tourn," the sheriff would travel through his shire and preside over meetings of the courts of the hundreds, which were smaller sub-divisions of a shire. At these courts, representatives of the region would report on infractions of national regulations and other prohibited activity. As early as the twelfth century, powers of hundredal jurisdiction were falling into the hands of local lords, either through usurpation or direct grant, so that by the late thirteenth century it was not uncommon for lords to "play sheriff" in a limited way by having views of frankpledge in their courts. The title, "view of frankpledge," is itself ancient, referring to the tithing, or frank-pledge groups, into which the adult [i.e., twelve years of age and above] male population was divided from as early as the late tenth century. Tithing groups were to provide surety for their members ordered to perform certain obligations, to guarantee that members would appear in court when required, and, eventually, to report on illicit behavior by members of the group. For the frankpledge in general, see William A. Morris, *The Frankpledge System* (Cambridge, Mass., 1910). For royal jurisdiction in private hands, see Ault, *Private Jurisdiction in England*.

22. In the small market town of Ramsey, a curia was held alongside, or immediately following, a view of frankpledge, both being recorded on the same roll. Later, in the sixteenth century, the courts of Ramsey, although called courts baron, embraced everything from regulations of retailers to land

Introduction

It is because of their extremely broad scope that local court rolls have attracted a great deal of scholarly attention, especially in the last half-century. Their value as sources for the social and economic history of the medieval English countryside was emphasized as early as the end of the nineteenth century by the seminal historian F. W. Maitland,[23] but it was not until the eve of World War II that they were exploited in a bold and imaginative way by the Harvard sociologist George Casper Homans. His *English Villagers of the Thirteenth Century* was a genuinely path-breaking book: a study of peasant society, institutions, and customs drawn primarily from court roll entries.[24] After the war, court roll-inspired or court roll-influenced research continued in England, in the work of W. G. Hoskins and Rodney Hilton,[25] and in Canada with the work of J. Ambrose Raftis, who, in 1964, published his *Tenure and Mobility*, an examination of land-

---

transfers between villagers. See Edwin B. DeWindt, *The Court Rolls of Ramsey, Hepmangrove and Bury*, Fiche 1, p. 53 (Court Roll of 3 January 1289), and Fiche 2, pp. 325–43 (Leets with courts, 21 December 1350; 21 April 1352), Fiche 3, p. 649 et seq., and Fiche 4, p. 973 et seq.

23. Frederic William Maitland, *Select Pleas in Manorial and other Seignorial Courts*, Selden Society 2 (London, 1888).

24. George Casper Homans, *English Villagers of the Thirteenth Century* (Cambridge, Mass., 1940).

25. W. G. Hoskins, *The Midland Peasant: The Economic and Social History of a Leicestershire Village (Wigston Magna)* (London, 1965), and *Provincial England: Essays on Social and Economic History* (London, 1965); Rodney H. Hilton, *The Decline of Serfdom in Medieval England* (London, 1966), *The English Peasantry in the Middle Ages, Bond Men Made Free: Medieval Peasant Movements and the English Rising of 1381* (London, 1973), and *A Medieval Society: The West Midlands at the end of the Thirteenth Century* (London, 1966).

holding practices and geographical mobility among the peasantry of the Ramsey Abbey estates in the East Midlands and based exclusively on court roll evidence.[26] Today, a court roll-based historiography is in place on both sides of the Atlantic, and discussion continues among social and economic historians as to the best ways to use and interpret this truly crucial but often frustrating (and sometimes infuriating) body of material.[27]

I have said that court rolls, and the information they contain, are crucial documents for understanding medieval English peasant society and culture. This is because, unlike any other source, they embrace an astonishingly broad spectrum of human activities. To be succinct (i.e., to revert to the "laundry list" mode of exposition), court rolls open doors[28] to

---

26. *Tenure and Mobility: Studies in the Social History of the Medieval English Village* (Toronto, 1964).

27. See Zvi Razi, *Life, Marriage and Death in a Medieval Parish,* and also his articles on the methodology associated with Raftis and his associates ("The Toronto School's Reconstruction of Medieval Peasant Society: A Critical View," *Past and Present* 85 [1979], pp. 141–57, "Family, Land and the Village Community in Later Medieval England," *Past and Present* 93 [1981], pp. 3–39); J. Ambrose Raftis, ed., *Pathways to Medieval Peasants* (Toronto, 1981); Judith M. Bennett, "Spouses, Siblings and Surnames: Reconstructing Families from Medieval Village Court Rolls," *Journal of British Studies* 23 (1983), pp. 26–46; Lawrence R. Poos, "Life Expectancy and 'Age of First Appearance' in Medieval Manorial Court Rolls," *Local Population Studies* 37 (1986). pp. 45–52; Edwin B. DeWindt, *The Court Rolls of Ramsey, Hepmangrove and Bury*; and Lawrence R. Poos, *A Rural Society after the Black Death: Essex, 1350–1525* (Cambridge, 1991).

28. I almost wrote "windows," but that image has been appropriated by Drs. Richard M. Smith, Lawrence R. Poos, and Zvi Razi in their debate over the demographic value of court rolls. See Zvi Razi, "The Use of Manorial Court Rolls in Demographic Analysis: A Reconsideration," *Law and History Review* 3 (1985), pp. 191–200; Lawrence R. Poos and Richard M. Smith, "'Shades

12

how court roles are helpful

such areas of inquiry as: local government and law enforcement; custom and/or customary law; local industries (e.g., brewing, baking); crafts and trades (e.g., tanning, butchering, shoemaking, glovemaking, candle-making, tailoring, dying, fulling, weaving, retailing, victualing, transport, carpentry, stone masonry, blacksmithing, goldsmithing); family structure, function, and size; sexual behavior; domestic and village-wide violence; environmental and ecological sensitivities or preoccupations; economic stratification and/or poverty; geographical mobility; recreation and entertainment (e.g., tennis-playing, football, excessive drinking, voyeurism and eavesdropping, even—it could be argued—false raising of the hue and cry by adolescents).[29]

But if court rolls open doors onto these and other areas of inquiry, they do not necessarily push historians through them, or, if the doors are entered, they are not always found to lead into carefully organized and complete storerooms of information. This is because local court rolls are often simply enrollments of presentments of individual behavior, actions, "done deeds," with little or no additional explanation or commentary. To read, for example, in the court roll of Hemmingford Abbots of 1313 that Agnes the daughter of Nigel was amerced 3 *d.* for trying to push Matilda the daughter of Martin into a flaming bake oven is certainly an intriguing and exciting record of

---

Still on the Window': A Reply to Zvi Razi," *Law and History Review* 3 (1985), pp. 409–29; and Zvi Razi, "The Demographic Transparency of Manorial Court Rolls," *Law and History Review* 5 (1987), pp. 523–35.

29. For medieval sport, see John Marshall Carter, *Sports and Pastimes in the Middle Ages* (Lanham, 1988), and John Marshall Carter and Arnd Krueger, eds., *Ritual and Record: Sports Record and Quantification in Pre-modern Societies* (Westport, Conn., 1990).

Introduction

human conflict.[30] But just why this medieval English village version of a scene from Hansel and Gretel occurred is never revealed. Such laconic entries abound throughout local court rolls. Hues and cries are raised by villagers upon their neighbors, the latter are amerced, but the reason for the hue in the first place is too often unstated. Similarly, men and women are amerced for acts of "trespass," frequently with no further information supplied. Ale brewers are regularly amerced for brewing contrary to the assize of ale, but scores of entries reveal nothing specific. Was the price too high? Was the brew inferior or undrinkable? Is the amercement, in fact, virtually little more than a licensing fee, having little or no connection to actual infractions of the assize? In short, motives for action, background information necessary to provide a context into which an entry can be fit, even something seemingly as straightforward as precise identification of named individuals, are all too often missing.[31]

---

30. *PRO* SC2/179/17. "And they say that Agnes the daughter of Nigel tried to push Matilda the daughter of Martin into a flaming oven, for which Matilda justly raised the hue and cry upon Agnes. Therefore, etc., 3 d. Pledge: Angerius, son of Nigel."

31. Anyone who has worked with the public records of medieval England is aware of the problem of personal identification, a problem intensified by the generally small pool of Christian names drawn upon for personal names, and the frequent practice of Christian names being taken from those of the godparents at baptism. (For Christian names, see DeWindt, *Land and People in Holywell-cum-Needingworth,* pp. 184–85.) Such genuine and distinctive recorded names as Marmaduke Faluntby, Alice Featherfinger, and, especially, Felicia Genitalia, do not present many problems of identification, but, given the ubiquity of the Christian names John, William, Thomas, Simon, Robert, Alice, Agnes, Margaret, Matilda, and Christina, it is not always a foregone conclusion that, e. g., a John Smith of one year is the same John Smith of the next year. Often, there are other bits of information that make the identification process easier—names of spouses, parents, children, occupation, proper-

14

Introduction

What historians have in the court rolls are records of behavior, pure and simple; nothing more, nothing less.[32] This does not mean that attempts to "know" medieval common people as distinct—and distinctive—men and women are hopeless and doomed to failure, but it does mean that, at least so far, there is no way to produce a comprehensive "biography" of a medieval peasant. Instead of biographies, we have the medieval equivalent of a "rap sheet" on a lot of men and women from the thirteenth to the sixteenth centuries. Now, as any good police investigator knows, "rap sheets"—the raw bits of personal information based on behavior alone—can be extremely revealing and useful. But they do not tell everything, and they certainly do not furnish access to a person's *mind*—to what he or she thought, cared about, believed, loved, hated, feared, or dreamed. It may be true that behavior is a better guide to people and who and what they really are than volumes of memoirs, confessions, or personal

---

ty, consistency of behavior—but the historian cannot always assume 100 percent certainty.

32. The importance of this cannot be minimized. For one, the record of peasant activities found in court rolls often presents a picture of peasant behavior at variance with the picture of the peasantry found in the writings of medieval English common lawyers. The well-known descriptions of serfdom, or villeinage, and its liabilities are frequently contradicted by the village record. On the question of serfdom, see Paul Vinogradoff, *Villainage in England* (Oxford, 1892); Frederick Pollock and Frederic William Maitland, *History of English Law before the Time of Edward I*, vol. 1 (Cambridge, 1898), pp. 356–83, 412–32; William S. Holdsworth, *A History of English Law* (London, 1923), III, pp. 491–510; and Rodney H. Hilton, *The Decline of Serfdom in Medieval London* (London, 1969). See also Paul R. Hyams, *Kings, Lords, and Peasants in Medieval England: The Common Law of Villeinage in the Twelfth and Thirteenth Centuries* (Oxford, 1980); and John Hatcher, "English Serfdom and Villeinage: Towards a Reassessment," *Past and Present* 90 (1981), pp. 3–39.

Introduction

declarations, but historians, not being behavioral psychologists, would like to have the words of peasants themselves.[33]

Sometimes historians think they do have peasants' words, or at least a close approximation. Admittedly such instances are usually late, chronologically, for the medievalist, but anything is better than nothing. The documents that contain these words are generally products of the fifteenth and sixteenth centuries and come from the non-common law courts

---

33. Nor should this be seen as cause for despair. The difficulty of producing a biography of any medieval figure, even the most prominent, is very real. With all the documentary material available for individual kings, for example, a full-fledged biography—one that manages to get inside the mind of the subject and explore motivations based upon the subject's personal testimony—of any medieval monarch has so far proved illusory. Even when there has survived a remarkable body of "autobiographical" material, as in the case of the French logician, Peter Abelard, and his companion, Heloise—a relationship immortalized in Abelard's *Historia Calamitatum* (sometimes called, by medievalists, when no one is looking, "Nobody Knows the Trouble I've Seen") and the subsequent correspondence between Abelard and Heloise—there are historians who have questioned the authenticy of the texts themselves, suggesting that, being as revealing and moving as they are, they must be works of fiction created by an unknown literary genius. In the final analysis, it does not matter. If Abelard and Heloise wrote the letters attributed to them, we have a rare glimpse into human thought and feeling in the twelfth century. If they did not write them, whoever did has given us an equally rare glimpse into human thought and feeling in the twelfth century. If the latter is true, all it means is that any attempt at a biography of Abelard and Heloise is problematical. If it is incorrect, it means that we have an astounding view of two people and their deepest, personal feelings—but we are still unable to write a full-scale biography of either of them, unless we assume that a psycho-sexual relationship is the sum-total of the lives and experiences of a man and a woman living in twelfth-century France. For Abelard, see Betty Radice, ed., *The Letters of Abelard and Heloise* (Harmondsworth, 1974); Etienne Gilson, *Abelard and Heloise* (Toronto, 1960); and Barbara Newman, "Authority, Authenticity and the Repression of Heloise," *Journal of Medieval and Renaissance Studies* 22 (Spring, 1992), pp. 121–57.

Introduction

of England (e.g., Chancery, Star Chamber) and the Church, specifically last wills and testaments. In the former, *depositions* were taken of litigants and witnesses, wherein specific questions were asked, and the answers, given under oath, were written down by scribes, albeit in the third person (e.g., "He says that he did not see a cow" rather than "He said, 'I never saw no bloomin' cow!'"). Such depositions do present problems, to be sure, but they bear witness to a peasant articulateness that is not found in court rolls.

Wills are a different matter. Dictated to a scribe and written in the first person, they are perhaps the only examples of ordinary voices from the past speaking directly to us about things that mattered—family, friends, money, property, possibly even God.[34] It is probably fair to say that wills are the most *personal* documents coming from the peasant milieu of late medieval England. Obviously, not every peasant made a will, and it could be assumed that, in general, peasants who

---

34. Naturally, there is a controversy over the reliability of wills, especially regarding religious affiliation and zeal in the period following the Henrician reformation (post 1540). It has been argued that wills frequently followed specific *formulae* for preambles, and the preamble used for a will invoking God, or God and Jesus alone, or God, Christ, the Virgin Mary and all the Saints, was less the choice of the testator than of the scribe. (See, for example, Margaret Spufford, *Contrasting Communities: English Villagers in the Sixteenth and Seventeenth Centuries* [Cambridge, 1974], esp. pp. 55–56, 320–23; J. Scarisbeck, *The Reformation and the English People* [Oxford, 1984], esp. Chapter I; J. D. Alsop, "Religious Preambles in Early Modern English Wills as Formulae," *Journal of Ecclesiastical History* 40 [1989], pp. 19–27; and Clive Burgess, "Late Medieval Wills and Pious Convention: Testamentary Evidence Reconsidered," in Michael A. Hicks, ed., *Profit, Piety and the Professions in Later Medieval England* [Gloucester, 1990], pp. 14–33). Whatever may be the ultimate consensus on the question of preambles, it may be suggested that once past the first sentences in a will, what we read regarding disposal of goods and property are most likely the words of the testator himself or herself, not the scribe.

17

made wills were atypical, being men and women with property substantial enough to bequeath.[35] This is not an insignificant point, but it does not matter much for the purpose of this introductory and selective description of sources. What is important here is the simple fact that wills—however late in the chronology of the English peasantry—offer opportunities to the historian to get as close to individual peasants' minds as he or she is likely to get when relying upon the written sources presently available.

So far, *written* sources for examining the world of the medieval English peasantry have been emphasized. This is understandable, since historians depend on the written word for knowledge of the past and have done so for centuries.[36] But the

---

35. Although this assumption itself is based on another assumption—that most peasants were people of meagre means and resources. The economic stratification within peasant society revealed by account roll and, more importantly, subsidy roll information urges caution in making such a sweeping assumption. In addition, if the wills of the small market town of Ramsey are any indication, not every will-maker in sixteenth-century Ramsey was a person of significant substance or property, while some of the most economically and socially powerful residents of the town failed to make wills. On the Ramsey wills, see the forthcoming study of the town by the present writer and Anne Reiber DeWindt.

36. The *oral* transmission of information within a culture is a deeply-rooted and virtually universal tradition, but it is hard for the historian to apprehend it because it *is* oral and often not written down. Committing ideas or information to writing gives them a kind of permanence and stability that may indeed alter them in profound, subtle and even not-so-subtle ways, but which makes them accessible to a wider audience and consequently available for broader and more comprehensive analysis and criticism. Historians can acknowledge and try to catch glimpses of oral traditions, but they remain ignorant of their full range and content and consequently rely most heavily upon the written word. A good example of this is the body of law and/or custom associated with Anglo-Saxon England. Several compilations of texts survive from the sixth through the eleventh centuries, but no serious Anglo-

Introduction

written word cannot be taken as the only valid source of information on the past. As noted earlier, most medieval peasants did not write. Indeed, whole cultures are, or have been, marginally or minimally literate.[37] Others, while literate, have left languages that cannot at present be deciphered.[38] Even in the cases of fully literate societies whose languages are well known, it is obvious that not all aspects of human existence are committed to writing. Hence, the growing importance of archaeology as yet a third major source of information on earlier cultures and societies, standing on an increasingly equal footing with literary and record sources.

Archaeology itself is a relatively recent discipline, and it

Saxonist believes that the whole corpus of Anglo-Saxon law and custom is known to us. The written texts represent but the tip of an iceberg whose true size and shape cannot even be imagined. It is for this reason that future generations will benefit from recent, contemporary efforts to record—in some cases, quite literally, *via* tape recording—the memories of African villagers, victims of the Great Depression, and Holocaust survivors. See regular bibliographies in the journal *Oral History Review*. See also: Al'Amin Mazuri, "African Archives and the Oral Tradition," *The Courier* 38 (Fall, 1985), pp. 12–15; B. Jewsiewicki and V. Y. Mudimbe, "Africans' Memories and Contemporary History of Africa," *History and Theory* 32, no. 4 (1993), pp. 1–11; Tom Tiede, *American Tapestry: Evewitness Accounts of the Twentieth Century* (New York, 1988); Benjamin Appel, *The People Talk: American Voices from the Great Depression* (New York, 1982); Claude Lanzmann, *Shoah: An Oral History of the Holocaust* (New York, 1985); and Lucette Valensi, *Jewish Memories* (Berkeley, 1991).

37. E.g., in Europe, the early Germans and the Celts.

38. E.g., the "Linear A" script of the pre-Myceneaen inhabitants of Crete, and the Etruscans.

has grown and matured profoundly in a little over a century.[39] *Medieval* archaeology is even younger than its parent (or sibling, depending on one's choice of metaphor). It is frequently conducted—especially in Great Britain—under less than ideal conditions, with limited funding, so that excavations can take years of annual digging sessions and, at their conclusion, still not embrace the whole site.[40] Or, they must be carried out hurriedly, as "rescue" archaeology, where a significant site is literally unearthed accidentally in the course of erecting a modern building or road, and construction is postponed just long enough to permit scholars to extract as much significant information and as many artifacts as possible before the site is lost, buried beneath the basement of a new parking garage or bank or under a new highway.[41] Also, with

---

39. One has only to compare the meticulous, painstaking, and literal *sifting* of dirt (i.e., earth) characteristic of archaeology today to Belzonni's virtual bulldozing his way into royal tombs in Egypt's Valley of the Kings in the nineteenth century. See Brian Fagan, *The Rape of the Nile* (New York, 1992), *passim*. On archaeology in general, see Colin Renfrew and Paul Bahn, *Archaeology: Theories, Methods, and Practice* (London, 1991).

40. The most well-known example of this is the deserted village site of Wharram Percy in Yorkshire. Under the direction of Maurice Beresford and John Hurst, scores of volunteers and professionals excavated the site in forty years of annual, three-week sessions. When the site was closed in 1990, only some 6 percent of its territory had been explored. For Wharram Percy, see Maurice Beresford and John Hurst, *English Heritage Book of Wharram Percy: Deserted Medieval Village* (London, 1990), and esp. p. 14.

41. Recent examples include the discovery of a fouteenth-century burial ground in the center of London's financial district, and the Rose Theatre project on that city's south bank. Sometimes, the businesses or institutions whose own building schedules were disrupted by discoveries have attempted to preserve part of the site, incorporating it into their own structures. See Duncan Hawkins, "The Black Death and the New London Cemeteries of

Introduction

few exceptions, medieval archaeology has not managed to capture the public imagination the way the archaeology of the Classical Mediterranean or, most spectacularly, the archaeology of ancient Egypt has done. The discovery in the 1930s at Sutton Hoo of the burial mound of an East Anglian king of the seventh century remains one of the landmark events in British medieval archaeology, but however wonderful the grave goods of Sutton Hoo are, they have not achieved the almost fantastical status of the tomb of the Egyptian pharaoh Tutankhamen. Indeed, no one has even tried to suggest anything as romantic as "the curse of Sutton Hoo." Similarly, the recovery of the so-called "Bog People" from the peat bogs of northern Europe-virtually perfectly preserved (if somewhat leathery) bodies of sacrificial victims to Germanic gods some 2000 years ago—has not ignited any popular excitement.[42] Nevertheless, despite the absence of headline-grabbing discoveries of hitherto un-dreamed-of treasures, medieval archaeologists go about their business with passion, care, and determination, annually adding valuable information to our understanding of life in the medieval countryside and town.

Just what does archaeology add to all that has been learned from literary and record sources? First and foremost, *things*—lots of them (and most of them broken). In other

---

1348," *Antiquity* 64 (September, 1990), pp. 637–42; and Brian M. Fagan, "The Rose Affair," *Archaeology* (March/April, 1990), pp. 12–15, 76–77.

42. On Sutton Hoo, see M. Carver, *The Age of Sutton Hoo* (London, 1994), and also M. Carver, ed., *Sutton Hoo Research Committee Bulletins 1983–1993* (London, 1993). On the bog people, see P. V. Glob, *The Bog People: Iron-Age Man Preserved,* tr. Rupert Bruce-Mitford (London, 1969). For an English example, see Don Brothwell, *The Bog Man and the Archaeology of People* (London, 1986).

Introduction

words, artifacts, physical remains of human, animal, and plant life, virtually anything and everything that has been associated with human living and that, in one way or another, has been left behind, whether discarded, abandoned, or lost. From personal jewelry to cooking utensils, clothing to the foundation stones and floors of houses and other buildings, pieces of furniture to the contents of the human digestive tract as preserved in cess pits and medieval latrines, weapons and coin hoards to the skeletal remains of men, women, and children buried in medieval cemeteries, a knowledge of the very material conditions of rural life and agricultural practice has been created that, when joined to the documentary record of the past, adds a concrete, physical reality to the behavioral and tenurial realities presented in court rolls and accounts.

The Village of Warboys cum Caldecote

Having surveyed the major categories of source material for information on medieval English peasants, it is now appropriate to turn to a consideration of the specific sources that have been translated for this collection. Since the audience for this text is assumed to be primarily students of medieval history, nothing from a specifically literary text has been included. Further, since archaeology deals in artifacts and other physical remains, it is impractical to supply material from that discipline.[43] Therefore, only material from *record* sources is provided. As already suggested, these are the only written materials that permit some measure of personalized contact with specific men

---

43. Photographs of skeletons, pottery fragments, floor foundations, etc., could have been reproduced, but the accompanying text explaining them would have made this a much larger—and longer—publication. Besides—as luck would have it—the village finally chosen is one that has not been the object of any archaeological investigation to date.

Introduction

and women from the past, so this gives them a special importance.

The manor-village complex selected is that of Warboys cum Caldecote, located in the present county of Cambridge.[44] It is some eight miles northeast of the town of Huntingdon and approximately sixteen miles northwest of Cambridge. In the Middle Ages it was one of the manors held of the king by the Benedictine abbey of Ramsey, and I have chosen to limit my selection to one of the Ramsey Abbey estates because the latter was a complex of villages and towns concentrated in Huntingdonshire but extending throughout the East Midlands into Northamptonshire, Cambridgeshire, and Bedfordshire. In addition, these estates have been the object of extensive and varying study since the nineteenth century. This means that there is a substantial body of scholarly literature about the manors and vills of Ramsey Abbey—from studies of law to analyses of manorial and village economy and society—that students can use to help construct a context into which the records themselves can be placed.[45]

---

44. Until 1974, Warboys was in the county of Huntingdon, but in that year Huntingdonshire was dissolved and absorbed into Cambridgeshire. Caldecote was a smaller settlement alongside the main vill.

45. For example, J. Ambrose Raftis, *The Estates of Ramsey Abbey*, examines the entire manorial regime of the abbey from the tenth through the fifteenth centuries. Equally important, Professor Raftis has also produced a monograph on the village of Warboys itself—*Warboys: Two Hundred Years in the Life of of an English Medieval Village* (Toronto, 1974). Edward Britton's *The Community of the Vill* is a study of the nearby village of Broughton, while Edwin B. DeWindt examines the village of Holywell in *Land and People in Holywell-cum-Needingworth*. Anne Reiber DeWindt has studied the peasant land market in the village of King's Ripton ("A Peasant Land Market and its Participants," *Midland History* 4, nos. 3 and 4 [Autumn, 1978], pp. 142–59); M. Patricia Hogan has written extensively on the village of Wistow ("Medieval Villany: A Study in the Meaning and Control of Crime in an

Introduction

Another reason for choosing Warboys, however, was the desire to find a village where there was an overlapping or close convergence of different kinds of records. Happily, Warboys was such a village. Between 1294 and 1309 there have survived a description of labor services expected from villein tenants,[46] a private charter,[47] an account roll,[48] two successive court rolls,[49] and a collection of fines and entry payments by tenants to the abbey.[50] In addition, the two court rolls, between

---

English Village," *Studies in Medieval and Renaissance History,* 2nd series, 2 [1979], pp. 121–215, and "The Labor of Their Days: Work in the Medieval Village," *Studies in Medieval and Renaissance History* VIII [1986], pp. 75–186); Sherri Olson examines the village of Ellington in "Jurors of the Village Court: Local Leadership Before and After the Plague in Ellington, Huntingdonshire," *Journal of British Studies* 30 (July, 1991), pp. 237–56, and "'Families Have Their Fate and Periods': Varieties of Familial Experience in the Pre-Industrial English Village," in Edwin B. DeWindt, ed., *The Salt of Common Life: Individuality and Choice in the Medieval Town, Countryside and Church* (Kalamazoo, 1996), pp. 409–48. Barbara Hanawalt has investigated crime in the region in "Community Conflict and Social Control: Crime in the Ramsey Abbey Villages," *Mediaeval Studies* 39 (1977), pp. 402–23. Raftis, again, has probed questions of violence and also social structures in communities surrounding Warboys in "Social Structure in Five East Midland Villages," *Economic History Review,* 2nd. series, 18 (1965), pp. 83–100; "The Concentration of Responsibility in Five Villages," *Mediaeval Studies* 28 (1966), pp. 92–118; and "Changes in an English Village after the Black Death," *Mediaeval Studies* 29 (1967), pp. 158–77.

46. See *infra*; p. 43 (B.L. Add. Roll 34341).

47. See *infra*; p. 45 (B.L. Add. Ch. 34179).

48. See *infra*; p. 76 (B.L. Add. Roll 39795).

49. See *infra*; p. 47 (B.L. Add. Roll 34777) and p. 61 (B.L. Add. Roll 39756).

50. See *infra*; p. 87 (B.L. Add. Roll 39693).

Introduction

them, represent good, comprehensive examples of the nature, range, and scope of such records, at least as produced by the Ramsey Abbey courts.[51]

The history of medieval Warboys cum Caldecote can be succinctly summarized.[52] There was a settlement in the tenth century, for in 974 the grant of Warboys by Archbishop Dunstan to the newly-founded Ramsey Abbey was confirmed in a charter by King Edgar. The manor was listed in the Domesday survey of 1086, assessed at ten hides to the geld.[53] It remained a property of Ramsey Abbey until the monastery's dissolution in 1540, at which time it, together with the bulk of the abbey's estates, was purchased by Sir Richard Williams,

---

51. For court rolls from other parts of the country, see, for example, Sue Sheridan Walker, ed., *The Court Rolls of the Manor of Wakefield from October 1331 to September 1333* (Leeds, 1983). For selections from a wide spectrum of courts, see the forthcoming volume of Select Pleas in customary land law found in local court rolls edited by Professors Lloyd Bonfield and Lawrence Poos and to be published by the Selden Society. In addition, Anne Reiber DeWindt attempts to locate the courts of the town of Ramsey itself in the larger context of nationwide courts in a forthcoming study of the town being written by herself and the present author.

52. What follows is largely based upon the account provided in William Page, Granville Proby, and S. Inskip Ladds, *The Victoria History of the County of Huntingdon* (London, 1932), vol. 2, p. 242–46 (hereafter, *VCH*). For a more detailed study of the social structure of the village from the thirteenth to the fifteenth centuries and based on an extensive use of local court rolls, see J. Ambrose Raftis, *Warboys*.

53. Hideage figures are problematical. Originally—in the Anglo-Saxon period—a hide was considered the amount of land necessary to sustain a family, and the usual equivalent was 120 acres. By the end of the Anglo-Saxon era, however, hideage had become a fiscal term—an amount of land that was taxed at the rate of a hide. The present village of Warboys covers some 8400 acres, which suggests that the medieval hideage figure (10 hides X 120 acres = 1200 acres) cannot be taken as a useful guide to size. (See *VCH*, 2, p. 242.)

Introduction

alias Cromwell, great-grandfather of the future Lord Protector of England, Oliver Cromwell. The medieval history of Warboys was, to say the least, uneventful. It remained throughout the period a simple manor-village complex and played no role on the greater historical stage until the early 1590s, when the five daughters of Sir Robert Throkmorton, tenant of the manor site itself, were alleged to have been bewitched by the neighboring Samuel family, an incident that culminated in 1593 with the hanging of Alice Samuel, her husband John, and their daughter Agnes for witchcraft and for the murder of Lady Susan Cromwell, wife of Sir Henry Cromwell, lord of Ramsey.[54]

The Records of Warboys cum Caldecote

The first document translated below is a summary of labor services owed by villein tenants of the manor of Warboys. Villeins were personally unfree. Labelled variously as serfs, customaries, naifs, or just villeins,[55] they held properties from their lords that were, in law, always the lords'. Hence the one major liability of villein status—the inability to bring suit

---

54. For the witchcraft case, see Anne Reiber DeWindt, "Witchcraft and Conflicting Visions of the Ideal Community," *Journal of British Studies* 34 (1995), pp. 427–63. For an abridged, modern English version of the pamphlet published in 1593 about the case, see Barbara Rosen, ed., *Witchcraft in England, 1558–1618* (Boston, 1991).

55. Serfs, in Latin, *servi*; customaries, in Latin, *customarii*—i.e., persons holding land at the will of the lord by the custom of the manor (*ad voluntatem domini secundum consuetudinem manerii*); naifs, in Latin, *nativi*; and villeins, in Latin, *villani*.

Introduction

against one's lord over customary property in the royal courts.[56] In addition, villeins were subject to other liabilities, such as paying fines to marry off their daughters (*merchet*),[57] paying tallages to their lords, being required to pay for license to leave the manor (*chevage*), and having the lord exact heriot at death.[58] However, it remains an open question as to how often these liabilities were, in fact, imposed, how burdensome they were, or, equally important, to what extent they were confined to the personally unfree. Often such disabilities were attached to the parcel of land itself, not the person, so that—as a perusal of such documents as the Ramsey Abbey cartulary[59] or the

56. For villeinage in general, see Pollock and Maitland, *History of English Law before the time of Edward I*, 1: 356–83, 412–32; Vinogradoff, *Villainage in England*; Holdsworth, *A History of English Law*, 3: 491–510; Paul Hyams, *Kings, Lords, and Peasants in Medieval England: the Common Law of Villeinage in the Twelfth and Thirteenth Centuries*; and Hilton, *The Decline of Serfdom in Medieval England*.

57. On *merchet*, see Eleanor Searle, "Freedom and Marriage in Medieval England: An Alternative Hypothesis," *Economic History Review,* 2nd series, 29 (1976), pp. 482–86; Jean Scammell, "Wife-rents and Merchet," *Economic History Review,* 2nd series, 29 (1976), pp. 487–90; Paul A. Brand and Paul R. Hyams, "Seigneurial Control of Women's Marriage," *Past and Present* 99 (1983), pp. 123–33; Rosamund Faith, "Seigneurial Control of Women's Marriage," *Past and Present* 99 (1983), pp. 133–48; and Eleanor Searle, "A Rejoinder," *Past and Present* 99 (1983), pp. 148–60.

58. Heriot was rendered either in kind or in cash. On many manors it was a surrender to the lord of the deceased tenant's best beast.

59. William Henry Hart and Ponsonby A. Lyons, eds., *Cartularium Monasterii de Rameseia*, 3 vols. Rolls Series no. 79 (London, 1884; repr. 1965). (Hereafter cited *Carts.*, with appropriate volume and page reference.)

Introduction

Hundred Rolls of 1274/1279[60] reveals—freemen could, and did, hold properties that imposed villein labor services and other servile customs or payments upon them.[61]

It is not the purpose of this introduction, however, to wrestle with the thorny question of villeinage. Here it is a question of trying to put the document under discussion into a context. Produced in or around 1294,[62] it is a description of labor services that is a substantially abbreviated version of the listing of services in the extent of the manor composed in 1251.[63] According to the 1294 document, the manor contained a total of forty-three 1/4 virgates[64] in villeinage and thirty-four

---

60. *Rotuli Hundredorum tempore Henrici III et Edwardi I in Turr' Lond' et in curia receptae scaccarii Westm' asservati*, 2 vols. (London, 1818). (Hereafter cited *RH*, with appropriate volume number and page reference.)

61. Much of this was a consequence of the "depersonalization" of work services discussed by J. Ambrose Raftis in *Tenure and Mobility*, pp. 15–24. Some of the properties in question had obviously once been servile tenements, later converted or otherwise transformed into freeholds, with a remnant of the earlier services still attached.

62. The date is that assigned to it by the British Library's Department of Manuscripts.

63. See *Carts.*, I, pp. 305–20.

64. A virgate, also known as a "yardland," was a unit of arable land. Its size varied from place to place, even within the same estate complex. Thus, on the Ramsey Abbey estates virgates ranged from eighteen acres to forty acres in size. In Warboys, the virgate was a unit of thirty acres, although it must always be kept in mind that the acre mentioned in medieval agricultural texts was a *customary acre* and not necessarily the equivalent of the modern statute acre. For the customary acre, see Edwin B. DeWindt, *Land and People in Holywell-cum-Needingworth*, p. 32. See also George Casper Homans, *English Villagers of the Thirteenth Century* (1941; New York, 1970), p. 49.

Introduction

crofts (counting two half-crofts as one croft). In 1251, the extent lists figures that are quite close—thirty-seven full virgates and fifteen half-virgates, for a total of forty-four 1/2 virgates, and thirty-three messuages with crofts and two half-crofts, for an identical total of thirty-four crofts. In addition, in 1251 there were also five virgates held freely and eleven manses held for rents and labor services.[65] In terms of actual tenants, the 1294 document reveals nothing, but in 1251 there were 4 freeholders, 70 men and women holding virgates either singly or jointly, 5 half-virgaters, 35 crofters, and 11 manse-holders, for a total of 125 tenants. Given the general correspondence, therefore, between the number of *tenements* in 1251 and 1294, it is probable that a similar number of *tenants* was present in the latter year as in the former.[66]

As stated in the 1294 works' document, the villein tenant had to perform labor services for his holding. A virgate rendered three works, or *opera*,[67] a week for forty-four weeks out of the year, with four extra works to be performed during the same period. Tenants called maltmen or ploughmen performed four works per week, with four additional works. Crofts rendered one work per week. During the harvest season, however—from the beginning of August to the end of September—the work services increased, with virgates performing four works per week and five additional works, and the maltmen rendering four weekly works but ten extra works. Only crofts remained unchanged.

---

65. See *Carts.*, I, pp. 308–19.

66. A similar number of tenements is found in the 1279 Hundred Roll for Warboys. In that year, there were thrity-six full virgates in villeinage and fifteen half-virgates (i.e., forty-three 1/2 virgates). See *RH*, II, pp. 601–02.

67. The plural of the Latin word *opus*, meaning "work."

Introduction

The 1251 extent presents a somewhat different picture of labor services. First, it is much more detailed. The *opera* owed by a virgate take up almost four pages of printed Latin,[68] although the description includes customary rent payments and numerous examples of the kinds of specific works that could be required. Basically, the virgater performs three works in any week from Michaelmas to the harvest season, but with one significant difference: during that time, he is expected to plough every Friday, except Christmas.[69] During the harvest period, in 1294, virgates rendered four works per week, whereas in 1251 the same obligation required a virgater to work a full day (*per totum diem*).[70] Half-virgaters and holders of smaller tenements render the same services as expected of croftholders in the 1294 document, but with the same exception as for virgaters: during the harvest time, they are to work from dawn to dusk (*a mane usque ad vesperam*).[71]

The main difference between the two documents of 1251 and 1294, however, does not lie so much in variations in the degree of week-work demanded from tenants as in the natures of the documents themselves. The 1294 document is concerned primarily with setting down the bare essentials of work required and calculating the actual number of work units and their cash equivalent. In other words, it is a working document—the kind of memorandum an estate administrator (e.g., a reeve or bailiff) would keep to assist in making an account

---

68. See *Carts*, I, pp. 309–12.

69. *Carts.*, I, p. 310.

70. *Carts.*, I, p. 310.

71. *Carts.*, I, p. 310.

Introduction

of the annual quota of works and commuting some (or all) for money if desirable. The 1251 extent, in contrast, is not only a more comprehensive record; it is an enrolling of the custom of the manor, a text to be appealed to by both lord and tenants. It spells out not merely what a tenant must do and how he must do it, but it also makes clear just what he cannot be expected to do and also what the lord's responsibilities are. For example, during the harvest villein tenants were required to render what were traditionally, and euphemistically, called *precariae*, or "love boons." However, they expected to be fed for performing these extra services, and the 1251 extent specifies what food will be provided: at the first, a half-penny's worth of bread, together with ale, pottage, fresh meat, and cheese, and at all subsequent boons the same amount of bread, and also ale, fish, pottage, and cheese.[72] Similar examples could be given,[73] but what may be suggested is that the 1251 extent documents complex and customary sets of reciprocal obligations and responsibilities which temper the arbitrariness of lordship and come suspiciously close to an area that would much later be the subject of contract.[74]

---

72. *Carts.*, I, p. 311.

73. E.g., *Carts.*, I, p. 311: carting three wagon-loads of grain from specifically named fields constitutes one work (*opus*); Ibid., obligation to cart one wagon-load of hay at Warboys but only a half-load if the destination is Ramsey.

74. It is interesting that medievalists have long emphasized the contractual nature of feudal relationships among the aristocracy but have not seen a similar pattern existing at the lower level of society. This does not mean that the medieval manor is the birthplace of the modern labor union movement. All it means is that the kind of document under discussion here points to a society wherein custom has placed checks on an unrestrained and free-wheeling exercise of power. When the 1251 extent declares that after a year's

Introduction

The 1294 summary of works shows the medieval English peasant seen as a unit of production by the landlord. The next document in the translated set is a solitary charter from the year 1303,[75] one of only thirty-eight private charters surviving from the village between the mid-thirteenth century and the latter years of the sixteenth century.[76] In it, one Ralph, son of William le Milnere, grants to Ramsey Abbey a messuage and ten acres of arable land in Warboys with the service of a couple who presently hold the property from Ralph himself. The land is freehold, the service in question is the nominal annual rent of a rose, and Ralph has effected this grant as a type of medieval insurance policy, since, in return for his cession of the property to the abbey, he has been included in the never-ending cycle of prayers offered by the monks for their benefactors and other suppliants. Whether or not Ralph is a villein is unrecorded. The fact that it is not possible to tell his legal status from the text alone is not without significance.

---

illness, the virgater will no longer be relieved of work obligations (*Carts.*, I, p. 312), one cannot claim that herein lies an early version of short-term disability insurance, but it does indicate that the lord did accept the reality of illness and was willing to allow up to a year's respite from services, with the exception of ploughing and boon works, itself a further reminder that it was not personal *performance* that was crucial in fulfilling labor obligations but rather personal *responsibility* to see to it that the required work somehow and by someone did in fact get done. See Elaine Clark, "Medieval Labor Law and English Local Courts," *American Journal of Legal History* 27 (1983), pp. 330–53.

75. See *infra*, pp. 45 (B.L. Add. Roll 34179).

76. Specifically, there are only twenty-eight charters from Warboys preserved in the British Library, covering the time period 1303 to 1568, while only ten charters can be found in the Public Record Office (London), from the thirteenth through the fifteenth centuries.

Introduction

After all, freemen and villeins both could hold free property and often did. This text has been included simply because it is the only charter from the period, and it is perhaps fortuitous that it also offers an example of a grant of personal property to a religious house in return for spiritual favors and, as such, affords a brief glimpse of one aspect of medieval religious behavior.[77]

The next text in the collection to be discussed here returns to the world of medieval English estate management: the account roll of 1306/1307. Here the primary focus of attention is the manor itself, as a productive economic enterprise, and the peasant appears in the record as one of many sources of income, both animal and vegetable. There are seventy-three accounts surviving from Warboys between the years 1250 and 1556, but they are scattered so haphazardly over that 306-year period that any attempt to use them as a meaningful base for an extended and comprehensive study of the economic history of the manor and vill during the later Middle Ages would be foolhardy.[78] However, the roll for the accounting year 1306/1307 is a reasonable example of an account and shows the types of information on the peasantry that can be extracted

---

77. For a specific example of patterns of *aristocratic* pious giving through wills in fifteeth-century England, see Joel T. Rosenthal, *The Purchase of Paradise: Gift Giving and the Aristocracy, 1307–1485* (London, 1972).

78. For lists of the surviving rolls, see *Lists and Indexes of the Public Record Office: Ministers Accounts*, and *Index to the Charters and Rolls in the Department of Manuscripts, British Museum*. The roll translated below is one of only seven surviving from the entire reign of Edward I (1272–1307).

Introduction

from such a source.[79]

After a heading giving the name of the official making the account—in this case, William the reeve[80]—and the date, the account begins with the first of the two parts that made up virtually any medieval account roll: receipts, to be followed by expenses.[81]

The account itself begins with a statement of arrears—the amount of money still owed by the reeve from the last account. There then follows a multi-part section of rents and customary payments received from tenants at each of the eight payment

---

79. See *infra*, pp. 76 (B.L. Add. 39795). Accounting years ran from one feast of St. Michael the Archangel (29 September) to the same feast in the following year.

80. A reeve was a manorial official charged with the primary responsibility of managing the lord's estate as an agricultural concern. For a popular but still useful description of a reeve's duties, see H. S. Bennett, *Life on the English Manor: A Study of Peasant Conditions, 1150–1400* (Cambridge, 1937). For contemporary medieval descriptions of reeves, bailiffs, and other manorial officials and their duties, see Dorothea Ochinsky, ed., *Walter of Henley and other Treatises on Estate Management and Accounting* (Oxford, 1971).

81. For account rolls in general, nothing has been published in recent years to surpass the explanation of accounts, accounting practices and systems given by P. D. A. Harvey in his edition of the records for the Oxfordshire manor of Cuxham (*Manorial Records of Cuxham, 1200–1395* [Oxford, 1976]). A shorter, but extremely useful, discussion of accounts was provided by the same author in *Manorial Records,* Archives and the User, No. 5 (London, 1984), written as a handbook for neophyte researchers. In addition, the treatises on estate management edited by Dorothea Ochinsky contain valuable information on accounting practices (*Walter of Henley and other Treatises on Estate Management and Accounting*).

Introduction

dates falling throughout the year.[82] The rents include the annual *assize* rent—a nominal payment due from each tenement and having little relationship to the actual value of the property—as well as payments of sheriff's aid,[83] and several payments representing cash commutations of earlier payments in kind: i.e., *hennesilver, maltsilver, fyssilver*, wine silver, *hewethyr, wethersilver*.[84] Also included among the rents are payments for labor services commuted *en bloc,* whereby villein tenements were held for a flat, annual money rent (i.e., *ad censum*), instead of works.[85]

---

82. Technically, there were nine dates, but the Easter and Hokeday terms are essentially the same, the latter occurring on the second Tuesday after Easter.

83. See *infra,* n. 220.

84. For explanations of these rents, see *infra*, notes 115, 123, 125, 126, 130, and 132.

85. The practice of commuting labor services to money rents fluctuated in England during the Middle Ages. The early twelfth century witnessed extensive commutation, but in the thirteenth century, benefiting from the population explosion of the twelfth and thirteenth centuries, landlords turned to high farming, and labor services tended to be reimposed throughout the country. Given that return to "free" labor, it is perhaps not surprising that the mid-thirteenth century witnessed the compilation of so many manorial extents and inquests into, and written enrollments of, customs and services, of which the 1251 Warboys' extent is an example.

The main advantage of *ad censum* tenure to the tenant was being free of work services in return for what, with the passage of time, became a rent, fixed by custom, which ultimately had little relation to the value of the labor itself. The advantage to the lord was, first, that he could dispense with works when the market for agricultural produce was depressed, and, second, that he could always reimpose labor services when required, since the *ad censum* arrangement was not permanent and the very label *ad censum* was a constant reminder that the property was villein land normally owing work services. See J. Ambrose Raftis, "The Structure of Commutation in a

35

Introduction

After the rents and money payments, the account next lists the profits of sales, from individual work units (*opera*) to agricultural produce and livestock.[86] Finally, the receipts section of the account concludes with what could be called the "profits of lordship"—entry fines into property (*gersumae)* and the amercements and other fines levied in the manorial courts.[87]

The expenses section of this particular roll is short. In addition, it rather abruptly stops. There is no final reckoning recorded, wherein the total expenses are compared to the total receipts, with a declaration of profit or loss. All this raises the suspicion that this roll is incomplete.[88] Nevertheless, it at least still manages to give a sense of the structure of an account, and that is what matters here.

There are three major segments to the expenses half of the roll. In the first, the reeve accounts for allowances for unpaid rents and tithes, together with purchases of livestock subsequently sent to the abbot's kitchen in Ramsey.[89] The second and third segments consist of payments or allowances to the abbey's cellarer and sub-cellarer, a reminder that Warboys was a manor that was part of the food-farm system of the abbey,

---

Fourteenth-Century Village," in M. Powicke and T. Sandquist, eds., *Essays in Medieval History Presented to Bertie Wilkinson* (Toronto, 1969), pp. 282–300.

86. See *infra*, p. 80.

87. See *infra*, p. 83.

88. Unfortunately, the roll for the following year (B.L. Add. Roll 39889) is certainly incomplete: it begins in the middle of the accounting process, with no heading.

89. See *infra,* p. 84.

obligated to supply food for the monks at Ramsey.[90]

The final estate-oriented document translated below is a short list of fines and *gersumae*, or entry fines to property, covering the period 1309/1310.[91] Like the preceding account roll, it is a fundamentally manorial and seignorial document— serving as another reminder that the peasant's world was rarely completely divorced from its relationship to the landlord.

All the above records can be used by historians to construct profiles of the tenurial, labor, and rent commitments and obligations of peasants—as individual men and women, as family groups, or as representatives of other, specific categor- ies, i.e., laborers, officials, men, women. But, regardless of how the data contained in the records are used, the peasant portraits that emerge from these particular documents are primarily portraits of peasants as landholders or employees of the manor. The other parts of peasant life are barely hinted at by lists of work obligations, charters, accounts, and entry fines. To appre- hend those other parts of peasant experience requires adding another body of sources to the general pool, and foremost among those sources are the local village court rolls.

With the court rolls of Warboys the focus of attention shifts from records of estate management, in which the local inhabitants of the village appear primarily as tenants, to a body of records in which they are the dominant and principal actors. This is apparent at the very beginning of the first roll translated

---

90. The food-farm system was introduced onto the abbey estates in the late twelfth century. For a discussion of the system, see J. Ambrose Raftis, *The Estates of Ramsey Abbey: A Study in Economic Growth and Organization* (Toronto, 1957), p. 97.

91. See *infra,* p. 87 (B.L. Add. Roll 39693).

below.[92] After the heading, giving the name and type of the court and the date, there is a list of twelve names. These are the jurors, or "the sworn ones" (*jurati*). Chosen for the office by their neighbors, with possible input from the lord,[93] they represented the community in the court and were charged with the task of making presentments of personal offenses and violations of regulations and custom. Sometimes jurors also served on special investigative panels, or "inquests," called upon by the court to examine specific complaints or problems more closely. Often drawn from the ranks of the more affluent and powerful members of local society, the jurors may possibly be seen as constituting the nucleus of a form of local government.[94]

Following the jury list is the notice of the payment of capitage, or the head-tax. This was rendered by the several tithing groups[95] in lieu of the personal appearance in court of every adult male.

The next items of business represent a variety of interests. The orders to arrest specific individual villeins who have left

---

92. See *infra*, p. 45 (B.L. Add. Ch. 34179).

93. The Ramsey Abbey court rolls frequently speak of the jurors—and other officials—being "elected." What "election" means is not explained. In addition, sometimes men are "elected" by the homage (i.e., the residents), sometimes by "the lord" or by his "steward," and sometimes by both the homage and the steward. On the question of election in Ramsey village court rolls, see Edwin B. DeWindt, *Land and People in Holywell-cum-Needingworth*, p. 220, n. 142.

94. On the jury, see Anne Reiber DeWindt, "Local Government in a Small Town: A Medieval Leet Jury and its Constituents," *Albion* 23 (1991), pp. 627–54.

95. For the tithing, or frankpledge, group, see *supra*, note 21.

Introduction

the manor without license reflect the concerns of the abbot of Ramsey as a lord, although it should be noted that the main offence lay in failing to pay the required fee to leave and that the lord (i.e., the abbot) knows where the missing villeins are residing—two of them, in fact, in Ramsey itself, right under his nose—and yet seems to have little inclination or ability to do much about it. This is especially suggested when it is seen in the following court roll[96] that, after the passage of a year, nothing has been done about the matter, and the same people are still away.

The matter of fugitive villeins is followed by an order that the bailiffs of the bishop of Ely be consulted regarding property appropriations. Here there are possibly several interests involved: the lord's, because his land has been encroached upon; the lord as agent of the king, because the king's road has been narrowed; and the peasants themselves, because their field has been flooded and the road they use has been restricted. It is entries such as these that are especially tantalizing, because however much there is a temptation to see them as examples of seignorial concerns pure and simple, it is helpful to remember that it was not the abbot of Ramsey who would first notice that he was standing knee-deep in water in the open fields and find that particularly disturbing, but the local villager himself, whose livelihood was growing in that flooded field.

The entries that follow are again a mixed group. The first is a straightforward, interpersonal debt case between one woman and the executors of a will. The next harken back to the matter of villeins being off the manor, only now it is a matter of persons who have left *with* permission—and are obviously haphazard in paying for their licences.

---

96. See *infra*, p. 61 (B.L. Add. Roll 39756), and especially p. 62.

Introduction

The remaining entries that make up the roll are, again, a constant mixture of seignorial and local community business, from the wrongful taking of rushes from the lord's marsh, *leyrwite*,[97] wrongful cutting of trees in the lord's wood, to personal complaints of trespass and debts, instances of inter-personal violence and the raising of the hue and cry, and the *private* settlement of debts and other, unspecified matters through the securing of licenses of concord. This constant intermingling of different interests continues in the second court roll,[98] with the addition of the presentments by the ale-tasters of infractions of the assize of ale, thereby providing a brief glimpse at one of the more ubiquitous medieval English rural domestic industries, ale-brewing.[99] Throughout both rolls, however, it is the peasant presence that is most vivid, together with the variety of activities recorded: juror, craftsman, brewer,

---

97. Leyrwite: an amercement for sexual misconduct, levied upon female members of the village community. See E. D. Jones, "The Medieval Leyrwite: A Historical Note on Female Fornication," *English Historical Review* 107 (1992), pp. 945–53.

98. See *infra*, p. 61 (B.L. Add. 39756).

99. On brewing, and particularly the dominant role of women in the business, see Judith Bennett, *Women in the Medieval English Countryside: Gender and Household in Brigstock before the Plague* (Oxford, 1987). Dr. Bennett is currently completing a major study of medieval English brewing. For examples of her most recent work, see Judith M. Bennett and Maryanne Kowaleski, "Crafts, Gilds and Women in the Middle Ages: Fifty Years after Maria K. Dole," *Signs* 14 (1988–89), pp. 474–88; Judith M. Bennett, "Conviviality and Charity in Medieval and Early Modern England," *Past and Present* 134 (1992), pp. 19–41; and Judith M. Bennett, "Women and Men in the Brewers' Gild of London, ca. 1420," in *The Salt of Common Life: Individuality and Choice in the Medieval Town, Countryside, and Church*, ed. Edwin Brezette DeWindt (Kalamazoo, 1995), pp. 181–232. See also David A. Postles, "Brewing and the Peasant Economy: Some Manors in Late Medieval Devon," *Rural History* 3 (1992), pp. 133–44.

Introduction

surety, victim, batterer, debtor, lender, trespasser, sexually active—a wide world of human actions and types in which the landlord is but one player among many. Such documents allow investigation of village government, economy, interpersonal and inter-group relationships, crime and non-conformity in general, mobility, and inter-action with other communities both within and outside the region. When coupled with the records of estate management, mentioned above, as well as with other records, such as subsidy rolls, and—from a later period—wills and parish registers, together with information obtained from archaeology, it is possible to put together a clearer, more comprehensive picture of medieval English peasant life than could ever be possible from reliance on just one or two types of sources alone.

Editorial Method

In the texts below, the following symbols are used: Words or phrases enclosed in square brackets [ ] are additions to the text supplied by the editor. Words or phrases enclosed in parentheses ( ) are marginalia in the original manuscript, usually written along the left-hand side of the parchment membrane. Words or phrases that are illegible in the original are indicated here by [...]. Finally, in translating personal names from their Latin forms into English, I have chosen to modernize *Christian* names (i.e., "Joan" instead of "Johanna," "Geoffrey" instead of "Galfridus," "Ralph" instead of "Radulphus"), but I have left *surnames* exactly as they appear in the original text, including variant spellings when the names are repeated. I have done this for two reasons: first, because it is not always certain when a name is really a title (e.g., "Molendinarius" [miller], "Prepositus" [reeve]); second, because I feel it is important that students experience first-hand the haphazard and utterly unstan-

Introduction

dardized way in which names were recorded by medieval scribes.

Texts

B.L. Add. Roll 34341
Customary Works From Diverse Vills.
Warboys With Caldecote.[100]
Works.

In the vill of Warboys with Caldecote there are 36 virgates and one quarter [virgate] of land, and also seven virgates [belonging to] maltmen and ploughmen.[101] There are also 33 Monday crofts with two half-crofts. Of these, each virgate renders in any week during the 44 weeks between the feast of St Michael[102] and the Gules of August,[103] three works and four works more. And every maltman and ploughman renders in any week during the same period four works and four additional works. And every Monday croft renders in any week one work. And the total of all the works is 7222 works.[104]

Holidays

And a work in winter is worth a half-penny, while in summer a work is worth 3 *d.* and a farthing.   *interesting*

---

100. MS: WARDEBOYS CUM CAUDECOTE. The British Library has dated this roll 1294. The Warboys entry begins on membrane 4.

101. MS: *maltmanni et akermanni.*

102. 29 September.

103. 1 August.

104. Using the figures given here, the total number of works for the period in question should be 7686.

43

Texts: Customary Work Services

Autumn Works

Further, each of the aforesaid virgaters renders in each week between the Gules of August and the feast of St Michael four works and an additional five works. And each of the maltmen renders in any week during the same period four works and an additional 10 works. And each Monday croft renders one work per week during autumn.

B.L. Add. Ch. 34179
[Charter of Ralph Milnere of Warboys]

Let all those, both now and in the future, know that I, Ralph
son of William le Milnere of Warboys, have given, conceded
and by this, my present charter, confirmed to Lord John, by the
grace of God abbot of Ramsey, and to the convent of the same
place and to their successors, and to the church of St Benedict
of Ramsey, all the service of Hugh de Eydon and Matilda, his
wife, in which [...][105] they are bound for one messuage and 10
acres of arable land with appurtenances in the said vill of
Warboys, together with the homages, reliefs and escheats of the
said Hugh and Matilda and their heirs of the said tenement
when they occur, all the above mentioned services with
appurtenances to be had and held by the said lord abbot and
convent and their successors forever. For this grant, concession
and my present charter of confirmation, they have admitted me
into all the benefits and prayers of their house. And I, the said
Ralph and my heirs truly will warrant the said service, namely
one rose annually at the feast of the Nativity of St John the
Baptist,[106] together with the said homages, wardships, reliefs
and escheats, to the said lord abbot, convent and their successors, and the aforesaid church, forever against all mortals.
In witness of which, I have affixed my seal to this my present
charter, with the [following] witnesses: John de Brocton, Ralph
Noreys, Walter de Deen, John Unfrey, John de Hykeneye,
Stephen de Aula and John Gocelyne of Broughton. Dated at
Warboys, the Sunday before the feast of St John before the

---

105. The charter is damaged at this point.

106. 24 June.

45

Lateran Gate,[107] in the thirty-first year of the reign of King Edward, son of King Henry.[108]

how they measured the passage of time

---

107. 5 May. The feast itself fell on the next day, Monday, 6 May.

108. 1303.

B.L. Add. Roll 34777[109]
Warboys[110]
Warboys. Monday After the Feast of the Purification of the Blessed Mary[111] **Year of the Reign of King Edward and the 20th Year of the Abbot [John],**[112] **Before William Wassingle.**

[Jurors]
Richard son of Richard Harsyne[113]
Hugh Beneyt[114]
Robert Smart[115]

---

109. This is a badly damaged roll. The left margin is torn away in several places. The text itself begins in the middle of the "skin" side of the parchment membrane. Further, although the heading does not declare it to be a view of frankpledge, references in the body of the text to orders issued in the "penultimate view" clearly indicate that this is the roll of a view of frankpledge. The absence, therefore, of any record of infractions of the assize of ale—a regular feature of the view of frankpledge—is a further indication that this roll is incomplete.

110. MS: Wardeboys.

111. The regnal year is obliterated on the roll.

112. 8 February 1305.

113. In the extent of 1251, William Harsyne, along with two other men— Richard Harsyne and William son of John—was tenant of one virgate. See *Carts.*, I, p. 312.

114. In 1327, Hugh Beneyt paid 21*d* in the subsidy of that year on movable property worth 35 *s.* (*Public Record Office* E 179/122/4; hereafter, *PRO* E179/122/4). In the subsidy of 1332, he paid 2 *s.* on movable property valued at 30 *s.* (*PRO* E179/122/7).

115. In the subsidy of 1327, Robert Smart paid 2 *s.* on movable property valued at 40 *s.* (*PRO* E179/122/4).

47

Texts: Court Roll, 8 February 1305

Richard le Bonde[116]

Nicholas Lane[117]
Henry Semar[118]
Alban Semar[119]
John de Hykeneye[120]

---

116. Richard le Bonde was tenant of thirty acres of land, held at the will of the lord, and for which he paid the abbot of Ramsey 20 *s.* annual rent. (See *RH*, II, p. 602). Since the land is described as being held at the will of the lord (*ad voluntatem domini*), the property was most likely villein, or customary, land held for a money commutation of the labor services. Richard does not appear in subsequent royal, or "national," records, but there are two men with the surname Bonde in the 1327 subsidy of a 20th on movables: William, paying 6 *d.*, and Ralph de Bonde, paying 22 *d. ob.* (*PRO* E179/122/4). Also, in the 1332 subsidy of a 15th, William Bonde appears again, paying 12 *d.*, as does Ralph, paying 2 *s.* 6 *d.* A third Bonde—Stephen—also is recorded, paying 18 *d.* (*PRO* E179/122/7). Finally, there was a Simon Bonde holding a half-virgate in the extent of 1251. See *Carts.*, I, p. 318.

117. In the subsidy of a 15th in 1332, an Emma *in Venella* [i.e., in the Lane] paid 12 *d.* See *PRO* E179/122/7.

118. The Semar family had been in the village in the middle of the thirteenth century, when Geoffrey Semare was recorded in the Extent as holding a virgate with Cristina Gerolde (*Carts.*, I, p. 314). In the 1327 subsidy of a 20th on movables, William Semar paid 10 *d.*, and Roger Semar paid 10 *d.* (*PRO* E179/122/4). In the 15th of 1332, William paid 8 *d.*, and a Richard Semar paid 2 *s.* 4 *d.* (*PRO* E179/122/7).

119. See the previous note.

120. The Hikeneye, or Higeneye, family appears to have taken up residence in the village in the late thirteenth century, since it is not mentioned in the 1251 extent but does appear in the 1279 Hundred Roll. The surname means "of Higney," a manor attached to the town of Ramsey. The earliest member of the family recorded is William Higeneye, holding one messuage of a half-acre and twenty acres of land, as freehold, from a certain Bartholomew

Texts: Court Roll, 8 February 1305

John Clericus[121]
John Prat
Alan de Grendale
William Rolf

(13 *s.* 4 *d.*)
One mark as capitage.[122]

(Order)
It is ordered that Stephen son of Henry Faber,[123] dwelling at

---

de Hamme. (*RH*, II, p. 602.) William himself was a landlord, as Ivo de
Hirst [an ubiquitous tenant throughout the region at the time] held a
messuage of a half-acre and fifteen acres of land from him for 2 *s.* annual
rent, Robert Cocus held a messuage of a half-rod and ten acres of land from
him for 15 *d.* annual rent, and Amabel le Gardiner held a messuage of a
half-rod and ten acres of land from him and from Ivo de Hirst for annual
rents of 8 *d.* to William and 6 *d.* to Ivo (*RH*, II, p. 602). The family was
still present in the 1320s and 1330s. In 1327, Hugh Higeneye paid 6 *d.*
towards the subsidy of a 20th, and in 1332, Roger Hikeneye was assessed 8
d. on 10 *s.* worth of movables (*PRO* E179/122/4, E179/122/7).

121. Because the surname Clericus simply means "clerk" or "cleric," it is
always difficult to be certain of precise identification of individuals with
this name in the absence of substantial or convincing evidence. Whether or
not there was a family connection, an Alexander Clericus was tenant of a
messuage with croft in 1251 (*Carts.*, I, p. 315), a Geoffrey Clericus held a
half-virgate in villeinage in 1279 (*RH,* II, p. 602), and a John "Clerk" paid
10 *d.* on movables worth 12 *s.* 6 *d.* in 1332 (*PRO* E179/122/7).

122. The capitage, or, literally, "head tax," was a payment by the tithing
groups excusing every member from actually being present in court.

123. The surname Faber, like Clericus, is an occupational name, meaning
"Smith," and, as with Clericus, it is difficult to assign family membership to
people bearing this name unless there is sufficient evidence. Because the
Warboys records are not continuous from the mid-thirteenth century to the
early fourteenth century, it would be unwise to assume that all persons

49

Wistow, Robert Peres, dwelling at Ramsey, William Sculle,[124] dwelling there, Ralph Wrek, dwelling at Benwick, and Simon son of Bartholomew, dwelling at Elsworth, be arrested.

Further it is ordered that a discussion be held with the bailiffs of the bishop of Ely of Somersham regarding a purpresture made at Schortewold by the said bishop's men of Fenton by obstructing the water course and flooding the field of Warboys, and [another] purpresture which the said men made at Stonylond by ploughing and narrowing[125] the king's road, as presented in the penultimate view.

(Postponed)

It is determined by the jurors that Emma le Soper owes Roger Chose and Roger Botylt of Fenton and Geoffrey son of Robert Chose, executors of the will of the said Robert, 4 s. 10 d. for malt that the said Robert, while alive, sold Emma. Therefore, let her make satisfaction to them concerning the said money, and for unjust detention she is in mercy. Pledge: her body, in the custody of the reeve and the beadle. Postponed.

---

named Faber are related. With this caution in mind, then, it can be noted that an Agnes Faber was assessed 2 s. on movables valued at 30 s., and a Richard Faber was assessed 10 d. on movables valued at 12 s. 6 d. in 1332 (*PRO* E179/122/7).

124. A Richard Sculle was tenant of a messuage with a croft in 1251. See *Carts.*, I, p. 315.

125. MS: *arrando et artando....*

Texts: Court Roll, 8 February 1305

(Order)

It is ordered that Emma Gerold,[126] who married at Fenton without the lord's licence, be arrested. *this one is interesting*

(Order)

Geoffrey Wyth, John son of Thomas Bedell, Bartholomew Sperver[127] and William le Soper are to be distrained to be at the next court to find pledges for their payments of capons.

(Order)

William Herbert[128] is ordered distrained by two pounds of cumin to do the same, as is Thomas son of William by four horseshoes.

(6 *d.*)

6 *d.* from Stephen son of Richard le Boneyr for a hue and cry justly raised on him by Emma le Soper, as presented in the last view. Pledge: John le Ponder.

---

126. The Gerold family had been present in Warboys in 1251. In that year, both Cristina Gerolde and Richard Gerolde were tenants, the former holding a virgate with Geoffrey Semare, the latter holding a virgate with John son of William (See *Carts.*, I, pp. 314, 312). In 1327, four Gerolds paid towards the subsidy: Godfrey (16 *d.*), Richard (21 *d.*), Simon (6 *d.*), and William (18 *d.*) Simon was still present in 1332, when he paid 12 *d.* towards the 15th of that year (*PRO* E179/122/4, E179/122/7).

127. A Hugh Sperver held a messuage with croft in the village in 1251. See *Carts.*, I, p. 315.

128. The Herbert family had been present in 1251, represented in the extent of that year by Cecilia Herbert, tenant, with Nicholas son of Richemannus, of a virgate (*Carts.*, I, p. 313). In 1327 and 1332, Robert Herbert paid 18 *d.* towards the 20th and 2 *s.* towards the 15th, respectively (*PRO* E179/122/4, E179/122/7).

(6 d.)
6 d. from William Hobbe of Broughton, who carried away the neighbors' rushes beyond the marsh of Warboys, as presented in the last view. Pledge: the beadle.

(3 d.)[129]
3 d. from Richard Pakerel[130] for selling rushes outside the marsh before the established day.[131] Pledge: Ralph Fyne.[132]

(6 d.)
It is determined by the jurors that Alan Hangate falsely complained against Ralph Molendinarius.[133] Therefore, he is in mercy for 6 d. Pledge: the beadle.

(3 d.)
3 d. from Ralph Molendinarius for unjust detention of 12 d.

---

129. The dorse, or "hair" side of the parchment membrane, begins at this point.

130. William Pakerel held a virgate in 1251 (*Carts.*, I, p. 314), and a Benedict Pakerel was assessed 3 s. against 45 s. worth of movables in 1332 (*PRO* E179/122/7).

131. MS: *ante diem statutum.*

132. The Fyne [Fine] family was present in 1251. Robert Fine held one manse for 6 d. annual rent and works in that year (*Carts.*, I, p. 318). In the subsidies of 1327 and 1332, Margaret [*aka* Margery] was assessed 12 d. in the 20th of 1327 and 16 d. in the 15th of 1332 (*PRO* E179/122/4, E179/122/7).

133. Another occupational surname, meaning "Miller." A Nicholas Milnere (i.e., Molendinarius) was assessed 10 d. in the subsidy of 1327. In 1332, he was assessed 2 s., while a Godfrey Molendinarius was assessed 18 d. in the same year (*PRO* E179/122/4, E179/122/7).

from Alan de Hangate. Pledges: William Fyne[134] and John de Hykeneye.[135]

(Order)
Further it is ordered that Richard de Fryndale be distrained to answer [to a charge of] carrying away one oak sapling[136] from the lord's wood.

(3 *d.*)
3 *d.* from Richard Mowyne for carrying his rushes beyond the separate meadow of the lord at *Longewoldslade*.

(6 *d.*)
3 *d.* from Henry Lefhere for the same. 3 *d.* from Nicholas Edward for the same. Pledges: the one for the other.

It is determined by the jurors that Richard Pylche,[137] while he was the garcon of John de Terreford, both night and day habitually[138] cut down oak saplings in the lord's wood and took them to the house of Thomas son of Robert, and he did this

---

134. See *supra*, note 132.

135. See *supra*, note 120.

136. MS: *blectronem*.

137. The Pilche (*aka* Pelche or Pylche) family was present in the middle of the thirteenth century, when Ralph Pilche held a messuage with a croft and also another half croft (*Carts.*, I, p. 316). In 1327, an Emma Pilche paid 6 *d.* towards the subsidy, while in 1332 a John Pilche (i.e., Pelche) was assessed 8 *d.* (*PRO* E179/122/4, E179/122/7).

138. MS: *ex consuetudine*.

with the consent of the said John while he was warden of the said wood. Therefore, let the third day within Easter week be set aside [for resolving this matter], by the pledges of Robert Albyn,[139] Robert Agathe, Geoffrey Pylche,[140] Ralph Fyne, William Hy and Simon Puttoke.[141] Afterwards he made a fine of a half-mark by the same pledges.

(6 *d.*)

3 *d.* from William Wodereve for carrying his rushes beyond the lord's meadow.

3 *d.* from Roger Edward for the same. Pledges: the one for the other.

3 *d.* from William Raven[142] for a licence of concord with Alan Semar and his wife Cecily. Pledge: Thomas Raven.

[It is determined][143] by the jurors that Robert le Carter cut

---

139. A John Albyn was assessed 20 *d.* in the 20th of 1327, and 2 *s.* 6 *d.* in the 15th of 1332 (*PRO* E179/122/4, E179/122/7).

140. See *supra*, note 137.

141. Puttoks were present in 1251, in which year Alexander Puttok held one messuage with a croft (*Carts.*, I, p. 315). A Thomas Puttok paid 2 *s.* towards the 15th of 1332 (*PRO* E179/122/7).

142. The Raven family was represented in 1251 by Robert Raven, tenant of one and a half virgates, for 5 *s.* 3 *d.* annual rent, and also meadow (*Carts.*, I, p. 308). In 1327, Roger Raven was assessed 6 *d.* towards the 20th, Thomas Raven Jr. 2 *s.* 6 *d.* Robert Raven paid 10 *d.*, and William himself was assessed 4 *s.* In 1332, Robert Raven was assessed 20 *d.* for the 15th, and Roger Raven 2 *s.* 6 *d.* (*PRO* E179/122/4, E179/122/7).

down and carried away 13 oak saplings beyond the lord's wood. Therefore, for trespass [Robert is amerced] 2 *s.* Pledges: William Scut and John le Ponder.

(Order)

3 *d.* from the reeve and the beadle for not arresting Alice daughter of John le Ponder to answer [a charge] of losing the lord's chattels in the chapter and for making a fine for *leyrwite*.[144] Further, it is ordered that she be arrested. 3 *d.* from the same [men] for not arresting Agnes daughter of Ralph le Cuhyrd for the same. And it is ordered that she be arrested.

→ Sexual misconduct

(18 *d.*)

6 *d.* from Alice daughter of Juliana Sculle[145] for *leyrwite*. Pledge: Thomas Raven. 12 *d.* from Grace daughter of Richard Pakerel for the same. Pledge: Richard Pakerel.

3 *d.* from Alan de Grendale for a licence of concord with Avice de Hygeneye. Pledge: John Unfrey.[146]

6 *d.* from William Fyne for the same with the same. Pledge: John Unfrey. 6 *d.* from Richard le Bonde for the same with the

---

143. The left margin of the membrane is torn away at this point.

144. See *supra*, note 97.

145. For the Sculle family, see *supra*, note 124.

146. The Unfrey family probably traced itself back to a certain Hunfridus (i.e., Humphrey), whose son, William, is noted in the 1251 extent, where his heir held a virgate for 2 *s.* annual rent (*Carts.*, I, p. 308). In 1332, an Alice Umfray paid 12 *d.* towards the 15th of that year (*PRO* E179/122/7).

same. Pledge: [....][147]

John [....] is distrained by one bill for trespass in the marsh, and he has not justified himself. Therefore, let it be retained, and let more be taken until [he justifies himself].

It is determined by the jurors that Beatrice, wife of William Fot, struck and mistreated[148] the daughter of Richard Godwyne to her damages of 2 *d.*, which she shall pay her. And for trespass she is mercy for 3 *d.* Pledge: Robert Fot.

(Order)
It is determined by the jurors that Avice le Hykeneye damaged the gates and trees of John de Hygeneye with her cart, to John's damages of 3 *d.*, which she shall pay him. And for trespass she is in mercy for 6 *d.* Pledge for both [obligations]: William Fyne.

(6 *d.*)
It is determined by the jurors that John de Hygeneye owes Avice de Hygeneye two-hundred rushes valued at 10 *d.*, which he shall pay her. And for trespass he is in mercy for 6 *d.* Pledge for both [obligations]: [....][149]

3 *d.* from [...][150] because they did not distrain Robert Clericus to respond to William Scut. And it is ordered [?to distrain the

---

147. Membrane torn away.

148. MS: *male tractavit.*

149. The membrane is torn away at this point.

150. The membrane is torn away at this point.

said Robert][151] to answer the said William. And [...][152] is William's pledge for prosecuting the said Robert.

3 *d*. from [...][153] de Hygeneye for a licence of concord with Cecily Godwyne. Pledge: William Fyne.

(Order)
It is determined by the jurors that John le Ponder unjustly defamed Thomas Raven, the beadle, calling him useless in the lord's service and even more outrageous things, to his damages of 6 *d*., which he shall pay him. And for trespass, etc., 6 *d*. Pledge: Simon Gerold.[154] *slander, service to the lord*

It is determined by the jurors that John le Ponder falsely complained against Thomas Raven. Therefore, he is in mercy. Excused. Pledge: Reginald Beneyt.

It is determined by the jurors that John de Hykeneye falsely complained against John de Broughton. Therfore, he is in mercy for [?6 *d*.][155]

[...][156] acknowledges that he owes Richard Wodcok[157] and

---

151. The membrane is torn away at this point.

152. The membrane is torn away at this point.

153. The membrane is torn away at this point.

154. See *supra*, note 126.

155. The membrane is damaged at this point.

156. The membrane is torn away at this point.

Simon Gerold 2 *s.* for [...][158], which he bought from them. Therefore, let him pay them the money. And for unjust detention he is in mercy for 6 *d.* Pledges for both [obligations]: John Unfrey and Alan de Grendale.

(Order)

6 *d.* from Robert Mably for mowing too much upon the lord's demesne in the marsh, and, also, that, in mowing, he appropriated part of the lord's marsh to himself. Pledge: Ralph Fyne. And it is ordered that one bill seized upon Robert Lytemold be retained, and that more be taken until he justifies himself by answering the same [charge].

(6 *d.*)

6 *d.* from Nicholas Molendinarius for a licence of concord with Ralph Molendinarius. Pledge: Richard Nel.

3 *d.* from Richard son of Robert Gosse for cutting down and carrying away twigs from the lord's wood. Pledge: the beadle. 3 *d.* from Robert Edwyne for the same. Pledge: John

---

157. Richard was assessed 6 *d.* on 10 *s.* worth of movables in 1327, and 8 *d.* on the same in the 15th of 1332. In the former year, two other members of the family were also taxed: Emma, paying 2 *s. ob.*, and Godfrey, assessed at 2 *s.* Godfrey reappeared in 1332, paying 3 *s.* 6 *d.*, when, in addition to Richard, he was also joined by John Wodecok, paying 8 *d.*, and William Wodecok, assessed at 16 *d.* (*PRO* E179/122/4, E179/122/7). In addition, a Cristina Wodecok had been recorded in 1251 as holding a virgate of land (*Carts.*, I, p. 313).

158. The membrane is torn away at this point.

Berenger.[159] 3 *d.* from Roger de Thernyngge for the same. Pledge: Hugh de Eydon. And it is ordered that one bill seized upon Robert Gray of Needingworth be retained, and that more be taken until he justifies himself by answering the same [charge]. [...][160] from Avice de Hygeney. Pledge: Hugh de Eydon'. 6 *d.* from Richard le Longe[161] for the same. Pledge: William le [....][162]

he admits his wrong

John le Ponder acknowledges that he owes Richard Wodecok one ring of peas, which he shall pay him. And for unjust detention he is in mercy for 3 *d.* Pledge for both [obligations]: Robert Smart.[163]

Geoffrey Wodecok complains against William le Soper. Pledge for prosecuting: Richard Wodecok. And it is ordered that the

---

159. The earliest bearer of this surname was Richard Berengarius, tenant in 1251 of a half-virgate (*Carts.*, I, p. 314). John Berenger—who may, or may not, have been this same John—held one quarter of land with a messuage containing one rod of land, freely (*RH*, II, p. 602). In 1327, there were four other men with the same family name: two Roberts, assessed at 12 *d.* and 6 *d.*, respectively, and two Williams, assessed at 20 *d.* and 17 *d.*, respectively (*PRO* E179/122/4). The two Roberts and two Williams were still present in 1332, when they were assessed 8 *d.*, 12 *d.*, 16 *d.*, and 16 *d.*, respectively (*PRO* E179/122/7).

160. The membrane is torn away at this point.

161. No persons with this surname are recorded prior to this roll, but a Margery Longe, assessed at 18 *d.*, and a William Longe, assessed at 2 *s.* 1 *d.*, are listed in the subsidy for 1332 (*PRO* E179/122/7).

162. The membrane is torn away at this point.

163. Robert appears in both subsidies, paying 2 *s.* on 40 *s.* worth of movables in 1327 and 2 *s.* on 30 *s.* worth in 1332 (*PRO* E179/122/4, E179/122/7).

said William be distrained to answer Geoffrey at the next court.

use of first names

(6 d., order)

Thomas Raven sufficiently proved that Robert son of Robert Edward lost a sack of the said Thomas containing iron and other small items valued at 20 d., which sack, with its contents, he had handed over to [Robert] for safe-keeping in the vill of Ramsey on the feast of St Benedict,[164] and which sack he never received back. Therefore, it is determined that [Robert] shall pay him the said 20 d., and for unjust detention he is in mercy for [....][165] Pledge: the reeve.

---

164. Either 21 March (the feast of St Benedict the abbot) or 11 July (the feast of the Translation of St Benedict).

165. The membrane is torn away at this point.

B.L. Add. Roll 39756

View [of frankpledge] at Warboys, Wednesday, the Feast of Saint Edmund Bishop and Confessor, at the end of the thirty-fourth year and beginning of the thirty-fifth year of the reign of King Edward, and the twenty-first year of the Abbot John,[166] in the presence of William de Wassingle.

(Names of the Jurors)
Richard Catoun[167]
Alan de Grendale
John Segely
William Berenger[168]

Geoffrey Herbert[169]
Simon Lane[170]
Nicholas Bugge
Richard le Noble[171]

Geoffrey son of Cecily

---

166. 16 November 1306.

167. Richard Catoun (i.e., Caton) was the tenant of a messuage with a croft containing one acre in the 1279 Hundred Roll (*RH*, II, p. 602). A John Catoun was assessed 6 *d.* in the 1327 subsidy (*PRO* E179/122/4).

168. For the Berenger family, see *supra*, note 159.

169. For the Herbert family, see *supra*, note 128.

170. For the Lane family, see *supra*, note 117.

171. Another Richard Noble, together with a William Noble, held a virgate of land in 1251 (*Carts.*, I, p. 313). In 1327, a Godfrey Noble was assessed 18 *d.* towards the 20th (*PRO* E179/122/4).

William Wodecok[172]
Reginald Beneyt[173]
Richard Puttok[174]

(13 *s.* 4 *d.*)
They give 13 *s.* 4 *d.* as capitage, that they not be called individually.

(1 capon)
Further, it is ordered to arrest Stephen son of Henry Faber and Robert Peres, dwelling at Ramsey, William Sculle, dwelling there, Ralph Wrek, dwelling at Benwick, and Simon son of Bartholomew, dwelling at Elsworth, who withdrew from the lord's fee with their chattels.

(1 capon)
Further, it is ordered that a discussion be held with the bailiffs of the bishop of Ely of Somersham so that a purpresture made at *Schorte Wold* by obstructing the water course and a purpresture at *Stonnyland* [made by] ploughing the king's road by the men of Fenton be corrected.

(1 capon)
William Chapman gives the lord one capon annually at Easter while he exercises the office of butcher, by pledge of William Gerold.

---

172. For the Wodecok family, see *supra*, note 157.

173. For the Beneyt family, see *supra*, note 114.

174. For the Puttok family, see *supra*, note 141.

Texts: Court Roll, 16 November 1306

(1 capon)
William Prepositus[175] is the pledge of Geoffrey Wyth for paying the lord one capon annually while he dwells outside the lord's fee.

(1 capon)
John le Pondere is the pledge of Bartholomew Sperner for one capon annually for the same.

(1 capon)
Ralph Scut is the pledge of John son of Thomas Bedell for one capon for the same.

(2 pounds of cumin)
Ralph Egate is the pledge of William Herbert for paying the lord annually two pounds of cumin while he dwells outside the lord's fee.

(4 horseshoes)
John son of Walter is the pledge of Thomas son of William for paying the lord four horseshoes while he dwells outside the fee.

(Order)
Further it is ordered that Richard de Grendale be distrained to answer [the charge] that he carried away one sapling from the lord's wood.

(Order)
Further it is ordered that John Aude be distrained to answer

---

175. The word "prepositus" means "reeve." However, since it is not certain whether William's title is a surname or official title, or both, I have chosen to leave the word in its Latin form.

[the charge] of trespass in the marsh, and also Robert Lytemold for the same.

(Order)
Further it is ordered that one bill seized from Robert Gray of Needingworth, be retained and that more be seized until he justifies himself by answering a charge that he carried away willows and twigs from the lord's wood.

(6 *d*.)
6 *d*. from Emma Gerold for marrying without the lord's licence at Fenton. Pledges: John le Ponder and William Hy.

(6 *d*.)
6 *d*. from Nicholas Molendinarius[176] for a licence of concord with Alan de Grendale. Pledge: William Prepositus.

(6 *d*., order)
Richard Pylche[177] acknowledged that he struck and wounded Henry Pakerel[178] to his damages assessed at 18 *d*., which he shall pay him. And for trespass the said Richard is in mercy [for] 6 *d*. Pledges: John Ponder and Richard le Bonde.

(12 *d*.)
It is determined[179] by the jurors that Hugh Pakerel falsely

---

176. For the Molendinarius (*aka* Miller, Milnere) family, see *supra*, note 133.

177. See *supra*, note 137.

178. For the Pakerels, see *supra*, note 130.

179. MS: *convictum est*.

brought a complaint against Stephen Cychely. Therefore, he is in mercy [for] 6 *d*. Pledge: Nicholas Plumbe.[180] [Also], 6 *d*. from Henry Pakerel for the same. Pledge: Geoffrey son of Richard.

property

(6 *d*., order)
Robert Mory acknowledged that he killed Nicholas Kannt's hen, to his damages assessed at 2 *d*., which he shall pay. And for trespass, he is in mercy [for] 6 *d*. Pledge for both [obligations]: Nicholas Plumbe.

(6 *d*., order)
Richard son of Reginald acknowledged that he struck and wounded Richard atte Wode,[181] to his damages assessed at 30 *d*., which he shall pay. And for trespass he is in mercy [for] 6 *d*. Pledges: John Unfrey[182] and the beadle.

(Removed because [recorded] below)
Geoffrey Scut acknowledged that he broke an agreement[183] with Amice Bugge concerning one selion of land which he leased[184]

---

180. A Simon Plumbe was tenant of a half-virgate in both 1251 and 1279 (*Carts.*, I, p. 317; *RH*, II, p. 602). Nicholas himself was assessed 20 *d*. for the subsidy of 1327 and 18 *d*. for the subsidy of 1332 (*PRO* E179/122/4, E179/122/7).

181. Richard was tenant of a messuage with a croft of two acres in 1279 (*RH*, II, p. 602). In the same year, a Geoffrey AteWode also held a messuage and croft (ibid.).

182. See *supra*, note 146.

183. MS: *conventio*.

184. MS: *locavit*.

*women have at
least some rights*

to her as partial payment of his debt for her damages assessed at [blank], which he shall pay. And for breach of agreement he is in mercy [for] 6 *d*. Pledge: [blank]. And it is ordered that the said Amice shall have the said one selion of land until she harvested two crops.[185]

William Fyne[186] acknowledged that he owes William Gerveys and John Tannator 20 *d*., which he immediately paid. And for in unjust detention he is in mercy. Excused.

(3 *d*., order)
William Scut acknowledged that he owes William Hy 6 *d*., which he shall pay. And for unjust detention he is in mercy [for] 3 *d*. Pledge: Ralph Scut.

(18 *d*.)
3 *d*. from Grace Pakerel for being unwilling to serve the lord in autumn, as she had been warned. Pledge: the beadle. 6 *d*. from Alice Sculle[187] for the same. Pledge: Thomas Raven.[188] 3 *d*. from Matilda atte Wode for the same. Pledge: Richard Godwyne. [Blank] from Thomas Raven, pledge of Beatrice Kaye, for not having her to answer to the same. And it is ordered that the said Beatrice be distrained to answer. Later she

---

185. MS: "Et preceptum est quod dicta Amicia habeat dictam terram usque ad duas vesturas inde percepit." See *infra*, p. 73 and note 202, for the rewritten version of this case, in which Geoffrey's name is transformed into Godfrey.

186. See *supra*, 132.

187. For the Sculle family, see *supra*, note 124.

188. For the Ravens, see *supra*, 142.

came and made a fine of 3 *d.*

(6 *d.*)
6 *d.* from William le Nunne[189] for not coming to render the lord's carrying service as summoned. Pledge: the reeve.

interesting that it's a criminal offense

Richard de Pydel complains against Alan de Grendale. Pledges for prosecuting: Ralph Fynne and Simon Puttok. And it is ordered that the said Alan be distrained to answer Richard at the next court.

(Order)
Simon le Dekine complains against Matilda Pylche.[190] Pledge for prosecuting: Richard le Bonde.[191] Pledge for defending: Thomas Raven.

(3 *d.*)
3 *d.* from Walter Galewey for damage caused by his horses in the lord's meadow. Pledge: William Prepositus.

(12 *d.*)
12 *d.* from Thomas Toperhyl for destroying the lord's marsh at night and for removing and carrying away the lord's rushes and turves. Pledge: the reeve.

(12 *d.*)

---

189. William was assessed 12 *d.* for the subsidy of 1327 and 8 *d.* for the subsidy of 1332 (*PRO* E179/122/4, E179/122/7).

190. For the Pylche family, see *supra*, note 137.

191. See *supra*, note 116.

12 *d.* from William Fot for cutting twigs and willows at night in le Holt of Boylescroft to the lord's damages. Pledge: John de Hygeneye.[192]

(15 *d.*)
12 *d.* from William Fot for cutting willows in the lord's wood. Pledge: Ivo de Hyrst. 3 *d.* from Nicholas Kannt for the same. Pledge: Laurence Kannt.

(Order)
Richard Godwyne is the pledge of Andrew Godwyne, his son, to answer a charge at the next court that he entered the chamber of the woodward and took away sureties[193] without the woodward's licence. And Nicholas Kannt is the pledge of Andrew Kannt, his son, to answer for the same.

(Tasters)
Nicholas Plumbe and Simon Gerold,[194] tasters, say upon their oath that:

(2 *s.*)
Matilda Heryng regularly brewed and sold [ale] at a penny. Therefore, because she broke the assize [of ale], she is in mercy for 2 *s.* Pledge: her husband. She did not come, but she sent [her] gallon, pottle and quart.

(12 *d.*)

---

192. See *supra*, note 120.

193. MS: *vadia*.

194. For the Gerolds, see *supra*, note 126.

12 *d*. from Amice de Hygenhey for the same, regularly. Pledge: Nicholas Plumbe. She did not bring [her measures].

(18 *d*.)
18 *d*. from Agnes Byschop for the same, regularly. Pledge: Nicholas Plumbe. She brought a gallon.

(12 *d*.)
12 *d*. from Emma Pylche for the same, regularly. Pledge: William the reeve. She came and brought a gallon, pottle and quart.

(18 *d*.)
18 *d*. from Agnes Braciatrix for the same, regularly. Pledge: Simon Gerold. She brought a pottle and quart.

[Amercement] excused from Alice Wymarke for the same, four times and at a half-penny. Pledge: Nicholas Plumbe. She did not bring [her measures].

(12 *d*.)
12 *d*. from Beatrice Catun for the same, regularly, at a penny. Pledge: Nicholas Plumbe. She brought a gallon, pottle and quart.

(12 *d*.)
12 *d*. from Alice Godefrey for the same, regularly. Pledge: Nicholas Plumbe. She brought a gallon and quart.

(12 *d*.)
12 *d*. from Alice Catun for the same, regularly. Pledge: Simon Gerold. She brought a gallon and quart.

(12 *d*.)

12 *d*. from Margaret Chamun for the same, regularly. Pledge: Nicholas Plumbe. She brought a gallon.

(12 *d*.)

12 *d*. from Alice Brun[195] for the same, regularly. Pledge: her husband. She brought a gallon, pottle and quart.

(12 *d*.)

12 *d*. from Alice Dereworth for the same, regularly, at a penny and a half-penny. Pledge: her husband. She did not bring [her measures].

(12 *d*.)

12 *d*. from Alice Clere for the same, six times, at a penny and a half-penny. Pledge: Nicholas Plumbe. She brought a gallon, pottle and quart.

(Presentment; order)

The jurors present that Stephen Gagon is a common malefactor in taking and stealing the geese and hens of his neighbors. Therefore it is ordered that he be seized if he comes upon the lord's fee.

(6 *d*.)

And they say that Juliana le Bonde badly beat Matilda Fyne in her own home, for which Matilda justly raised the hue and cry upon her. Therefore, Juliana is in mercy for 6 *d*. Pledge: William Prepositus.

[handwritten margin note: multiple notes between violence between women]

---

195. The Brun (i.e., Broun, Bronne) surname is found in the 1327 and 1332 subsidies in the person of Henry Broun, assessed 20 *d*. to the 20th and 3 *s*. 6 *d*. to the 15th (*PRO* E179/122/4, E179/122/7).

And[196] the aforesaid jurors say that Richard Pylche badly wounded Henry Pakerel with his knife, for which the said Henry justly raised the hue and cry upon him. Therefore, Richard is in mercy for 12 *d*. Pledge: Reginald Beneyt.

(6 *d*.)

And they say that Stephen the son of Cecily beat and mistreated[197] Hugh Pakerel, for which the said Hugh justly raised the hue and cry upon him. Therefore, the said Stephen is in mercy for 6 *d*. Pledge: Simon Puttok.

(Order)

And they say that John the son of Hugh de Eydon struck and mistreated Alice Derworth, for which the said Alice justly raised the hue and cry upon him. And because the said hue and cry was not taken up,[198] the whole vill is in mercy, as it appears below. And the said John is ordered distrained to answer.

(6 *d*.)

And they say that Richard the son of Reginald struck and mistreated Richard atte Wode, for which the said Richard justly raised the hue and cry upon him. Therefore, the said Richard [son of Reginald] is in mercy for 6 *d*. Pledge: John de Hygeneye.

---

196. The dorse side of the membrane begins here.

197. MS: *male tractavit*.

198. MS: *non fuit prosecutum*.

And they say that Henry de Broughton, servant of the farmer[199] of Wolneye took away and, with his cart, carried off the forage of Richard Plumbe, for which Adam, the servant of the said Richard, justly raised the hue and cry upon the said Henry. And because the said hue and cry was not taken up, the whole vill is in mercy, as it appears below. And the said Henry is ordered distrained to answer.

(13 *s*. 4 *d*., order)
And they say that Alice Pylche badly beat Joan Grubbe, for which Joan justly raised the hue and cry upon her. And because the said hue and cry was not taken up, the whole vill incurs a fine for all [the said derelictions] of 13 *s*. 4 *d*. And Alice is ordered distrained to answer.

(Order)
And they say that Emma the daughter of Richard Gosse married in the bishopric of Ely without the lord's licence. Therefore, let her be arrested if she comes [upon the fee].

(18 *d*.)
And they say that Alice Sculle was convicted in the chapter of fornication. Therefore, she is in mercy for 12 *d*. Pledge: Reginald Beneyt.

4 *d*. from Grace Wynter for the same. Pledge: John Unfrey.

---

199. MS: *firmarius*. A farmer was one who took up property for a fixed rent, and who then recouped his outlay from the profits of the land. If he was lucky, he received more than he had paid in rent. If he was unlucky, he ended up with a loss.

(6 *d*., order)

And they say that Emma Fyne badly gleaned in autumn. Therefore, etc., for 6 *d*. Pledge: William Fyne. And Denise[200] Cler is ordered distrained for the same, and also Matilda Pakerel and Emma Hy.

(Order)

And they say that Philippa Sperver[201] regularly carried away and stole the grains of the lord and the neighbors in autumn. Therefore, she is ordered distrained to answer.

(6 *d*., order)

Godfrey Scut came and acknowledged that he broke an agreement with Amice Bugge concerning one selion of land which he rented to the said Amice for four years as partial payment of his debt of one cow. Therefore, he is in mercy for 6 *d*. And because it is determined by the jurors that no customary can dismiss or rent any part of his servile land to anyone except for a term of two years, according to the custom of the manor, the said selion is ordered seized into the lord's hand until, etc.[202]

(2 capons)

Two capons from Richard Neel at Easter while he dwells at Ramsey. Pledge: Richard Neel.

---

200. MS: *Dionisia*.

201. For the Spervers, see *supra*, note 127.

202. MS: "capiatur in manu domini donec etc." For an earlier version of this case, see *supra*, note 185, where Godfrey is recorded as "Geoffrey."

(1 capon)

One capon from Robert son of Ralph Edwyne at Easter while he dwells outside the lord's fee. Pledge: Robert Smart.

(27 hens)

Four female woodcocks[203] from William Hy for having a decoy[204] in the lord's wood. Four hens[205] from William Semar[206] for the same. Four hens from Alexander Tixtor for the same. Four hens from Roger de Hygeneye for the same. Four hens from Henry Brun[207] for the same. Four hens from Ralph son of Alan for the same. Four hens from Richard son of Ralph for the same.

(1 capon)

One capon from Richard Pylche at Easter while he dwells at Bury. Pledge: Reginald Beneyt.

(5 capons)

One capon from John son of Thomas while he dwells outside the fee. One capon from Ralph Wrek for the same. One capon from Geoffrey Wrench for the same. Two capons from Bartholomew Sperver for the same.

---

203. MS: *gallinas silvestras.*

204. MS: *pro uno volatu in bosco domini habendo....*

205. MS: *gallinas.*

206. For the Semars, see *supra*, note 118.

207. See *supra*, note 195.

Texts: Court Roll, 16 November 1306

(1 capon)
One capon from Geoffrey Wrench for one cottage that he holds
from William Lucas.

(3 capons)
Two capons from John le Ponder while he exercises the office
of butcher. One capon from William le Soper for the same.

(2 pounds of cumin)
Two pounds of cumin from William Herbert[208] while he dwells
at Hilton.

we can learn about what they ate

(4 horseshoes)
Four horseshoes from Thomas son of William while he dwells
at Pidley.

(2 capons)
Two capons at Easter from Richard Egath while he dwells at
Huntingdon. Pledges: Robert Egath and William Prepositus.

---

208. See *supra*, note 128.

B.L. Add. Roll 39795
Warboys, in the twenty-second year of the Abbot John.[209]
Account of William Prepositus of Warboys, from the Feast
of St Michael, in the twenty-second year of the Abbot
John,[210] **to the same feast the following year.**[211]

[RECEIPTS]
(Arrears)
He renders account of 52 *s*. 5 *d*. *ob*.[212] *q*.[213] of his arrears of the
last account.

Total: 52 s. 5 d. ob. q.

(Michaelmas)[214]
He renders account of 8 *s*. 9 *d*. *ob*. of assize rent.
[He renders account] of 10 *s*. from Richard le Bonde[215] for the
land of Roger Clericus, and 16 *s*. 8 *d*. from the mill at farm.

Total: 35 s. 5 d. ob.

---

209. 1306. Abbot John began his tenure of office in 1285, dying in 1316.

210. 29 September 1306

211. 1307.

212. *ob.=obolum*, or a half-penny.

213. *q.=quaterium*, or farthing [one quarter of a penny].

214. The Michaelmas accounting term, beginning at the feast of St Michael,
29 September [1306].

215. See *supra*, note 116.

(Term of St Martin)[216]

He renders account of 2 *s.* 11 *d.* of *hennesilver*.[217] And 13 *d.* are missing from four ploughmen, two wardens of the assart and from Wolfeye.[218]

Total: 2 *s.* 11 *d.*

(Term of St Andrew)[219]

He renders account of 3 *s.* 7 *d.* of assize rent, 8 *d.* of the remainder of the sheriff's aid,[220] 20 *s.* from six virgates of land *ad censum*, with each paying 40 *d.*, 5 *s.* from six crofts *ad censum*, with each paying 10 *d.*, 16 *d.* from two half-crofts *ad censum*, with each paying 8 *d.*, and 16 *s.* 8 *d.* from the mill at farm for this term.

---

216. 10 November [1306].

217. *Hennesilver* was one of the many customary rents rendered by tenants to their lords on medieval English estates. This particular rent was apparently a money commutation of an earlier payment in kind, namely in hens. For the subject of customary rents in general, see Nellie Neilson, *Customary Rents*, in Paul Vinogradoff, ed., *Oxford Studies in Social and Legal History*, vol. 2 (Oxford, 1910).

218. Wolfeye was a place in Warboys, apparently a cultivated area or field. See *Carts.*, I, pp. 307, 311.

219. 30 November [1306].

220. Sheriff's aid, or *auxilium vicecomitis*, was money paid by virtually all tenants—free and unfree—on the estates of the abbey of Ramsey. Originally intended to assist the sheriff in meeting his expenses while performing his duties, by the late thirteenth century it had become a royal payment, usually by-passing the sheriff altogether. On the Ramsey estates, however, because of the extensive powers enjoyed by the abbots, the money was kept by the abbot. The rate itself varied from 2 *d.* to 6 *d. q.* per virgate. See Neilson, *Customary Rents*, pp. 92, 124 et seq.

[Further, he renders account] of 12 *d*. from Roger atte Wode[221] for three acres of land recently in assart,[222] 4 *d*. from the same Roger of new rent for one acre of land in assart, 12 *d*. of new rent from Simon Gerold[223] for three acres in assart, and 8 *d*. new rent from Thomas Brown for two acres there.

Total: 50 *s*. 3 *d*.

(Term of the Purification of Blessed Mary)[224]
He renders account of 14 *s*. 7 *d*. of *Hewethyr*.[225] And 15 *d*. are missing from the reeve, the beadle, the warden of the marsh and two wardens of the assart.

Total: 14 *s*. 7 *d*.

(Term of the Annunciation)[226]
He renders account of 3 *s*. 7 *d*. of assize rent, 8 *d*. of the remainder of the sheriff's aid, 16 *d*. *fysilver*,[227] 3 *s*. of wine

---

221. For the AtteWode family, see *supra*, note 181.

222. Assart refers to land recently brought into cultivation from waste, marsh or even woodland.

223. See *supra*, note 126.

224. 2 February [1307].

225. This is a customary rent that cannot be identified. It could be associated with a money payment in place of animals [i.e., wether], or it could refer to a payment for a right to cut wood [i.e., hew...].

226. 25 March [1307].

227. *Fysilver*, a monetary substitute for an earlier payment of fish to the abbot, to meet his needs during Lent. See Neilson, *Customary Rents*, pp. 33–34.

silver,[228] 16 *s*. 8 *d*. from the mill at farm, 20 *s*. from six virgates *ad censum*, and 6 *s*. 8 *d*. from six crofts and two half-crofts. Also, 12 *d*. from Roger atte Wode for three acres of land recently in assart, 4 *d*. from the same Roger for one acre of land recently in assart, 12 *d*. from Simon Gerold for three acres in assart, and 8 *d*. from Thomas Brown for two acres.

(Easter Term)[229]
He renders account of 6 *s*. 9 *d*. assize rent, and 10 *s*. from Richard le Bonde for the land of Roger Clericus.

Total: 71 *s*. 4 *d. ob*.[230]

(At Hokeday)[231]
He renders account of 14 *s*. 2 *d*. of *Hewethyr*. And 13 *d*. are missing from the reeve, the beadle, the warden of the marsh, and two wardens of the assart. [Further, he accounts for] 8 *s*. 9 *d*. of *maltsilver*,[232] and 15 *d*. are missing from the woodward.

Total: 22 *s*. 11 *d*.

---

228. Wine silver, the commutation for a money payment of service in the vinyard. See Neilson, *Customary Rents*, pp. 58–59.

229. Easter Sunday: 26 March [1307].

230. The scribe has combined the totals for both the Annunciation and Easter terms.

231. The second Tuesday after Easter [i.e., 4 April 1307].

232. *Maltsilver*, a commutation for a money payment of an earlier obligation to provide malt to the abbey's brew house. See Neilson, *Customary Rents*, p. 36.

(Term of St Benedict)[233]

He renders account of 3 *s.* 7 *d.* assize rent, 13 *s.* 9 *d. Hewethyr*, with 11 *d.* missing from the reeve, beadle, warden of the marsh, and two wardens of the assart, and 8 *d.* as remainder of the sheriff's aid. Also, 2 *s.* 10 *d. ob. q.* of *wethersilver*,[234] with 1 *d. ob.* missing from the reeve, beadle and warden of the marsh, 20 *s.* from six virgates of land *ad censum*, 6 *s.* 8 *d.* from six crofts and two half-crofts *ad censum*, 16 *s.* 8 *d.* from the mill at farm, 12 *d.* from Roger atte Wode for three acres of land recently in assart, 4 *d.* from the same Roger [for one acre of land], 12 *d.* from Simon Gerold for three acres, and 8 *d.* from Thomas Broun for two acres.

Total: 66 *s.* 10 *d. ob. q.*

(Term of the Nativity of Blessed Mary)[235]

He renders account of 12 *s.* received from the men of Broughton for licence to mow in the marsh of Warboys.

Total: 12 *s.*

(Works sold)

He renders account of 52 *s.* for 1048 works sold from the feast of St Michael[236] up to Hokeday,[237] the price of each work being a half-penny, and of which 20 *s.* comes from the time of

---

233. 11 July [1307].

234. *Wethersilver*, a commutation for money of an earlier payment of a wether to the abbot's flock. See Neilson, *Customary Rents*, pp. 42, 82.

235. 8 September [1307].

236. 29 September.

237. The second Tuesday after Easter.

Gilbert.[238] Also, 76 *s.* 8 *d.* for 920[239] works sold from Hokeday[240] up to the feast of St Michael,[241] except for five weeks in autumn, (with the price of each work being 1 *d.*) Also, 27 *s.* for 215 works sold in autumn during five weeks, with the price of each work being 1 *d. ob.*[242]

Total: £7 15 *s.* 8 *d.*

(Wheat[243] sold)
He renders account of 4 *s.* for two rings[244] of corn sold to the stackers[245] and winnowers,[246] and 4 *s.* 4 *d.* for two rings also sold to them.

---

238. The meaning of this reference is unknown. Gilbert could refer to a previous tenant or even to a previous monastic official.

239. Ramsey Abbey's scribes employed the so-called "long hundred" in their accounts, whereby C—normally the Roman numeral for 100—equalled 120.

240. The second Tuesday after Easter.

241. 29 September.

242. The figures here do not add up properly. 215 works (using the Ramsey Abbey long 100 for C) sold at 1*d. ob.* each would yield a total of 26 *s.* 10 *d. ob.*, not the scribe's 27 *s.*

243. MS: *Frumentum,* the Latin word for "wheat," which the British call "corn."

244. Ring: a unit of measurement equivalent to four bushels.

245. Stackers, i.e., persons employed to stack the harvested grains.

246. Winnowers, i.e., persons employed to winnow the harvested grains.

(Barley sold)

He renders account of 16 *d.* for three bushels of barley sold to the winnowers.

(Peas sold)

He renders account of 9 *d.* for three bushels of peas sold to the winnowers.

Total: 10 *s.* 5 *d.*

(Stock sold)

He renders account of 53 *s.* 4 *d.* for 16 pigs sold to the Cellarer,[247] with the price of each pig being 3 *s.* 4 *d.* Also, 48 *s.* for 12 pigs sold to William Talbard of Broughton, the price of each pig being 4 *s.* Also, 9 *s.* 8 *d.* for two pigs sold to an associate of the same William, 6 *s.* for two pigs sold to William Baynard, 24 *s.* for eight pigs sold to John le Ponder, 4 *s.* for one pig sold to the same, 18 *d.* for one calf sold to him, 15 *d.* for one calf sold to him, 10 *s.* 6 *d.* for two pigs sold to William Chapman, and 2 *s.* from the sale of one very old and worn out[248] cart horse.

Total: £8 3 *d.*

(Dead stock sold)[249]

He renders account of 5 *s.* for 70 cheeses sold after the feast of St Michael, 21 *d.* for three and a half gallons of butter, the price of each being 6 *d.*, 2 *s.* for 24 cheeses, 24 *s.* for 31

---

247. The Cellarer was the abbey official reponsible for the provisioning of the abbey.

248. MS: *debilis.*

249. The dorse side of the membrane begins here.

sheepskins, 21 *d.* for two lamb skins and one pellet,[250] and 8 *d.* for one-wool-fell.

(Small Items sold)

He renders account of 3 *s.* 2 *d.* from the sale of apples, 7 *d.* for the sale of 32 doves, nothing from the sale of underwood, 14 *s.* 1 *d.* from the sale of pannage,[251] and 4 *s.* from the profits of the marsh.

Total: 57 *s.*

(Fines and *gersumae*)

He renders account of 5 marks received from William Segely as gersuma for one virgate of land formerly his father's, 5 *s.* from Alice Segely for licence to marry, 13 *s.* 4 *d.* from Ralph Buk for one croft formerly Henry le Sopere's, 3 *s.* 4 *d.* from William son of Albin for one messuage and a half-rod of land formerly Albin Semar's,[252] 40 *s.* from Geoffrey Gerold for a half-virgate formerly his father's, [unrecorded] from Sarah Swan[253] for having entry into one cottage formerly Hawise Swan's, 5 *s.* for the heriot[254] of Matilda wife of Simon

---

250. MS: *pellecta.* A shorn or plucked pelt.

251. Pannage refers to the right to allow pigs to forage.

252. See *supra*, note 118.

253. A Thomas Swon was assessed at 16 *d.* for the subsidy of 1332 (*PRO* E179/122/7).

254. A heriot was the payment, either in livestock or cash, rendered to the lord upon the death of a tenant holding customary, or servile, land.

Margaret[255] of Caldecote, 40 s. from Geoffrey son of Bartholomew for having entry into a half-virgate of land formerly his father's, 4 s. from John son of William Thurkyl for having entry into one cotland formerly Nicholas Albyn's[256], and 40 s. from John le Rede[257] for having entry into a half-virgate of land formerly Richard Wodecok's.[258]

Total: £10 18 s. 4 d.

(From the view [of frankpledge] and other courts)
He renders account of 66 s. 2 d. from the view [of frankpledge], 7 s. 3 d. from the court held on the feast of the apostles Philip and James,[259] and 49 s. 9 d. from the autumn court.

Total: £6 3 s. 2 d.

Total of all receipts with arrears:
£52 13 s. 8 d. ob.

(EXPENSES)
He accounts for an allowance in the lord abbot's chamber of

---

255. The Margaret, or Margery, family was represented by a Robert Margaret/Margery in the subsidies of 1327 and 1332, paying 2 s. 3 d. and 3 s., respectively (*PRO* E179/122/4, E179/122/7).

256. For the Albyns, see *supra*, note 139.

257. John paid 10 d. towards the subsidy of 1327 and 20 d. towards the subsidy of 1332 (*PRO* E179/122/4, E179/122/7).

258. See *supra*, note 157.

259. I.e., 1 May.

the rent of Richard le Bonde: 20 *s*., by two tallies.[260]

He accounts for an allowance in the same chamber of 50 *s*. from the view [of frankpledge], by one tally.

He accounts for an allowance in the same chamber of 10 *s*. of tithes, by one tally.

He recently rendered account at Christmas at the abbot's kitchen for one calf, three piglets and 16 ducklings from stock.

[He renders account] of 12 *d*. for one goat bought and sent there at Easter, and of 9 *d*. for 12 pullets bought and sent there at the same time.

[He renders account] of 21 *d*. for one calf bought and sent to the lord at London at parliament before the beginning of Lent, and also for 12 goats from stock.

Total: £4 3 *s*. 6 *d*.

(Cellarer)
He renders account of payments to the cellarer of £4 upon a tally. And he paid him 64 *s*. for eight allowances of hard cheese; also for two allowances from stock, and 120 *s*. for 10 allowances of bacon. [Further, he renders account of] 66 *s*. for frestynges,[261] 4 *s*. 10 *d*. for lambs, 2 *s*. for beef, 6 *s*. 8 *d*. for mutton, 16 *s*. 4 *d*. for butter, 6 *s*. 8 *d*. for herring, and 12 *s*. for fresh cheese.

---

260. A tally was a wooden stick upon which notches were carved, indicating the amount of money either received or owed by the holder of the tally.

261. I.e., postponed debts.

(Sub-cellarer)[262]

[He renders account of] 4 *s.* paid to the chaplain of the lord abbot, 10 *d.* in the tailor shop, 8 *d.* in the brew house, 3 *s.* to the sub-cellarer for wine making, by one tally, and 8 *s.* for honey paid to the receivers,[263] by one tally.

Total: £18 15 *s.* 8 *d.*

---

262. Sub-cellarer, a monastic official subordinate to the cellarer.

263. The precise identity of these "receivers" is unclear, but, most likely, it is a reference to individuals employed by the abbey to collect payments from its various estates.

B.L. Add. Roll 39693

Gersumae and fines made to the abbey of Ramsey from the Feast of St Michael,[264] in the twenty-fifth year of the Abbot John, up to the same feast the following year.[265]

Warboys

4 s. from Henry Semar[266] for the marriage of his daughter Alice.

41 s. from Henry Brun[267] for having entry into a half-virgate of land through Joan Gosse.[268]

18 d. from Agatha daughter of Henry Isabel for licence to marry.

4 s. from Christina daughter of Nicholas Basely for licence to marry.

Richard Magely gives the lord 40 s. *gersuma* for a half-virgate of land once belonging to his father, which land William, younger brother of the said Richard, previously surrendered into the lord's hands to the use of the said Richard.

---

264. 29 September.

265. 1309–10.

266. See *supra*, note 118.

267. See *supra,* note 195.

268. The Latin text reads as follows: "De Henrico Brun pro ingressu habendo ad Johannam Gosse in dimidia virgata terre xlj s." A literal translation would be: "41 s. from Henry Brun for having entry into Joan Gosse in a half-virgate of land," which, for all its titillating indelicacy, is actually a quite accurate statement of the facts.

William Folke of Warboys gives the lord a half-mark[269] *gersuma* for one cottage of Agnes Top.

It is determined that in past times it was customary in the vill of Warboys with Caldecote that if any customary tenant of the lord died holding land without an heir by him and his wife, then the lord would receive all the goods, movable and immovable, as much as from the deceased as from his widow, found on the day he died, and a third part of the said goods, according to the aforesaid custom, would remain in the power of the lord, equally and fully. And such is the custom as much after the death of the wife as after the death of the husband should they end their days without any legitimate heir. And therefore it is determined and conceded that the aforesaid custom shall henceforth be fully observed in all things in the said vill. And concerning this, upon the death of Richard Plumbe,[270] who held a virgate of land, [and who died] without an heir by himself and his wife, his widow Matilda came and made a fine with the lord for 5 marks[271] for the said custom.[272]

---

269. I.e., 6 *s.* 8 *d.*

270. See *supra*, note 180.

271. I.e., £3 5 *s.* 1 *d.*

272. This text is also inserted into the Ramsey cartulary, where, in the printed edition, it is appended to the main text as a footnote. See *Carts.*, I, p. 307, n. 1.

Glossary

Ale, Assize of. A national regulation of the brewing trade requiring that ale sold for consumption be both drinkable, sold by accurate measures, and priced in accordance with the current selling price of the cereal ingredients.

Assart. A piece of land, variable in size, recovered from previously uncultivated land, such as waste or marsh.

Bailiff. A manorial official, frequently charged with collecting rents for the landlord or exercising other administrative responsibilities, including the oversight of the agricultural and pastoral activities of the manor. Sometimes a salaried employee, in contrast to the Reeve [q.v.], who was usually a villein and rewarded with rent reductions or a tenement.

Beadle. A manorial official, subordinate to and often assisting the reeve or bailiff.

Bill. A tool, used for pruning, trimming, or cutting, consisting of a long blade with a concave edge, often having a hook at the end.

Bread, Assize of. A national regulation of the baking trade, requiring that bread sold for consumption be of the proper weight, quality, and priced in accordance with the current costs of the relevant grains.

Capitage. Literally, "head tax." A cash payment rendered by villein tenants of a manor excusing their personal appearance in courts at views of frankpledge.

Glossary

Cellarer. A monastic official responsible for the provisioning of a monastery.

Censum, ad. Land held for labor services which have been commuted to an annual money rent.

Concord, license of. An out-of-court agreement between two or more individuals settling a debt or other matter initially moved as an item of litigation. A license of concord usually involved the payment of a fee to the court by the party seeking the licence.

Croft. A small piece of arable land, sometimes, but not always, next to a house.

d.[=denarius]. A penny. This was the standard unit of money in England in the late thirteenth and early fourteenth centuries.

Demesne. The arable property of a manor retained by the lord for his own use. land for the lord
Glebe. land for the church
Distraint. The act of seizing and retaining, by court order, a piece of movable property from an individual as a means of enforcing compliance with an order. The distrained property, often called a "distress," was returned upon the proper fulfillment of the responsibility.

Escheat. The right of a lord to confiscate property held by a free tenant found guilty of a felony.

Farmer [firmarius]. A person holding property, whether small or large [e.g., a manor], for a fixed money rent paid to a

90

superior but then having the right to collect and retain all rents or dues from the property, even if the amount collected is in excess of the rent paid.

Farthing [q.=quarterium]. A monetary unit; one-quarter of a penny. In the late thirteenth and early fourteenth centuries, farthings were frequently literally a quarter piece of a silver penny, just as a half-penny was often exactly that—one-half of a silver penny.

Firmarius [farmer]. See *Farmer.*

Frankpledge, view of. A court held annually by a sheriff in the hundred court in his circuit of the county or, especially by the thirteenth century, by a manorial lord including the right to oversee the activities of the members of local tithing [*q.v.*] groups and the enforcement of the assizes of ale and bread [*q.v.*].

Frestynges. Postponed debts.

Fysilver. A monetary payment to the lord of the manor as a substitute for an earlier payment of fish to meet the lord's needs during the season of Lent.

Gersuma. An entry fine, i.e., payment by an incoming tenant to the lord for permission to take possession of a tenement.

Hennesilver. A customary rent, originally a payment of hens to the landlord, later commuted to a money payment.

Heriot. A payment by the widow of a servile tenant to the lord upon the death of her husband, often being a surrender of the deceased's best beast but frequently commuted into a money payment.

Hewethyr. A customary rent, specific meaning unknown, but most likely involving sheep.

Homage. The act whereby a tenant acknowledged his dependent status vis-à-vis his lord. Frequently joined to the act of fealty, wherein the tenant swore to be faithful to his lord and his lord's interests. Also, a general term used in court rolls to describe the entire dependent peasant population.

Hue and Cry. A peace-keeping institution, whereby anyone witnessing the commission of an illicit act by another person was required to cry out and initiate a pursuit, which was to be taken up by all other residents of the community.

self-governance

Leyrwite. A monetary penalty imposed on servile female villagers for fornication.

Maltsilver. A customary rent; originally a payment of malt to the lord, later commuted into a money payment.

Messuage. A piece of land, varying in size, but large enough to accommodate a dwelling.

Opus, ad. Literally, "at work"; the term used to describe servile tenure held for the performance of labor services.

Pannage. A payment by tenants for the right to let their pigs forage in the woods.

Pellet. A shorn or plucked pelt.

Glossary

Pledge. A personal surety. An individual who guarantees the appearance in court or performance of an obligation by another.

Pottle. A half-gallon liquid measure.

Prepositus. See *Reeve.*

Purpresture. A piece of land illicitly appropriated from the land of another or from royal roads.

q. [quarterium]. See *Farthing.*

Reeve [Prepositus]. An official charged with responsibility for the economic and agricultural management of a manor, similar in function to a bailiff, except that reeves were often of villein or servile status and were usually not paid a salary but were instead released from labor services and/or granted a piece of land.

Relief. Monetary payment by the heir to a freehold tenement, paid to the feudal lord for permission to enter into the property.

Ring. A unit of measure equalling four bushels.

s. See *Shilling*

Selion. A narrow strip of land of variable length lying between two furrows in the open field.

Serf. A man or woman of servile status. Also called Villein, or Naif.

Glossary

Sheriff's aid. A customary rent paid by all Ramsey Abbey tenants, free or unfree, assessed on virgate holdings at a rate varying from 2 d. to 6 d. q. per virgate and originally intended to help pay the expenses of the sheriff while performing his duties.

Shilling [=s.]. A monetary unit, consisting of 12 d. There were 20 shillings to the pound. There was no shilling coin in the late thirteenth and early fourteenth centuries.

Sub-Cellarer. Monastic official, assistant to the cellarer [*q.v.*]

Tally stick. A narrow piece of wood in which notches were cut indicating payments and/or receipts.

Taster [ale]. Village official responsible for enforcing the assize of ale [*q.v.*]

Tithing. A group in rural society consisting of ten or more males twelve years of age and older responsible for producing its members in court and for reporting illicit acts by group members to the sheriff or his representative at the annual view of frankpledge [*q.v.*]

Villein. A serf [*q.v.*]

Virgate. A unit of arable land, varying in size from eighteen acres to over forty acres. The "average" virgate was a thirty-acre unit of land.

Warrant. A guarantee of right to property, provided by the donor or seller to the receiver or purchaser of a piece of free

Glossary

land. Once property had been "warranted," the tenant had the right to alienate the property.

Wethersilver. A customary rent, originally the payment of a wether to the lord's flock but, by the late 13th century, commuted into a money payment.

Wine silver. A customary rent, substituting a money payment for personal service in the lord's vineyard.

Suggested Readings

The Medieval English Countryside

Any attempt to understand the world of medieval English peasants should begin with the physical world they inhabited. Still a stimulating book, although a little dated in the light of research that the author himself set in motion, is W. G. Hoskins, *The Making of the English Landscape* (London, 1955). More recent introductions to the countryside of medieval England can be found in Grenville Astill and Anne Grant, *The Countryside of Medieval England* (Oxford, 1988); Leonard Cantor, *The Changing English Countryside, 1400–1700* (London, 1987); and Brian K. Roberts, *The Making of the English Village: A Study in Historical Geography* (Harlow, 1987); while an especially valuable series, The Making of Britain, which attempts to see the history of England and the history of the land itself as inseparable, includes the excellent volume by Trevor Rowley, *The High Middle Ages, 1200–1550* (London, 1988). On the question of early village settlement and the origins of the village itself, Brian K. Roberts, *Rural Settlement* (London, 1987), is a good place to start, while more specialized studies will be found in Michael Aston, David Austin, and Christopher Dyer, eds., *The Rural Settlements of Medieval England: Studies Dedicated to Maurice Beresford and John Hurst* (Oxford, 1989).

The Medieval Manor and the Rural Economy

Most peasants in medieval England lived either on or in some relationship to a manor, and the best place to start

Suggested Readings

examining the history of the manor is still the pioneering work by Frederic William Maitland, *Domesday Book and Beyond: Three Essays in the Early History of England* (Cambridge, 1897). Equally valuable is Paul Vinogradoff, *The Growth of the Manor* (Oxford, 1911). Much more recent scholarship on the question largely consists of extended footnotes to those two books. However, when attention turns to the nature and history of the rural economy of medieval England, the literature is vast and, apparently, never-ending. Two excellent general introductions are M. M. Postan, *The Medieval Economy and Society: An Economic History of Britain, 1100–1500* (Berkeley, 1972) and J. L. Bolton, *The Medieval English Economy, 1150–1500* (London, 1980). On medieval English agriculture, there is the on-going series *The Agrarian History of England and Wales,* published by Cambridge University, of which seven of a projected eight volumes have already appeared. H. E. Hallem, *Rural England, 1066–1348* (Brighton, 1981), is a useful general survey of the economy of the countryside prior to the Black Death, which can be supplemented by the essays in Bruce M. S. Campbell, ed., *Before the Black Death: Studies in the "Crisis" of the Early Fourteenth Century* (Manchester, 1991). For the beginning student, clear introductions to specific subjects are: David Hall *Medieval Fields* (Aylesbury, 1982); Warren O. Ault, *Open-Field Farming in Medieval England: A Study of Village By-laws* (London, 1972); and Christopher Dyer, *Standards of Living in the Later Middle Ages: Social Change in England, c. 1200–1520* (Cambridge, 1989). A valuable collection of essays and studies is M. M. Postan, *Essays on Medieval Agriculture and General Problems of the Medieval Economy* (Cambridge, 1973), while one of the genuine landmarks of modern scholarship on medieval agricultural society is Evgeny Alekseevich Kosminsky, *Studies in the Agrarian History of England*, trans. Ruth Kisch, ed.

Suggested Readings

Rodney H. Hilton (Oxford, 1956), a book that is also one of the single greatest cures for insomnia ever produced.

Medieval English Peasant Society

H. S. Bennett, *Life on the English Manor* (Cambridge, 1937), although seriously dated, remains one of the best general introductions to the medieval English peasant's world available to the curious reader. Two books that illustrate the importance of village court rolls as a source for peasant history are George Casper Homans, *English Villagers of the Thirteenth Century* (Cambridge, Mass., 1940) and J. Ambrose Raftis, *Tenure and Mobility: Studies in the Social History of the Medieval English Village* (Toronto, 1964). Among more recent studies, stimulating essays on peasant society and culture will be found in Richard M. Smith, ed., *Land, Kinship and Life-cycle* (Cambridge, 1984) and J. Ambrose Raftis, ed., *Pathways to Medieval Peasants* (Toronto, 1981). Judith M. Bennett, *Women in the Medieval English Countryside: Gender and Household in Brigstock before the Plague* (Oxford, 1987) provides a good examination of women's experience in the medieval village, while Barbara A. Hanawalt, *The Ties That Bound* (Oxford, 1986) is an extremely readable and sound portrait of the medieval English peasant family and its environment. Alan Macfarlane, *The Origins of English Individualism* (Oxford, 1978), is a serious book that challenges the very appropriateness of the term "peasant" as applied to England at all and should be read alongside the same author's *The Culture of Capitalism* (Oxford, 1987), in which he answers the many critics of his thesis. All the works of Rodney H. Hilton are worth reading, but especially recommended are his *The English Peasant in the Middle Ages: The Ford Lectures for 1973, and*

Suggested Readings

Related Studies (Oxford, 1975); *Bond Men Made Free: Medieval Peasant Movements and the English Rising of 1381* (London, 1973); and a collection of essays, *Class Conflict and the Crisis of Feudalism: Essays in Medieval Social History* (London, 1985). For the question of serfdom, or villeinage, Rodney H. Hilton, *The Decline of Serfdom in Medieval England* (London, 1966), is valuable, while the legal implications of villein status are explored in Paul R. Hyams, *Lords and Peasants in Medieval England: The Common Law of Villeinage in the Twelfth and Thirteenth Centuries* (Oxford, 1980). The broader legal world of the peasant, specifically his relationship to the various courts in medieval England, can be explored through John S. Beckerman, "Procedural Innovation and Institutional Change in Medieval English Manorial Courts," *Law and History Review* 10 (1992); Helen M. Cam, *Liberties and Communities in Medieval England* (New York, 1963); Anne Reiber DeWindt, "Local Government in a Small Town: A Medieval Leet Jury and its Constituents," *Albion* 23 (1991); Edwin Brezette DeWindt, *The Court Rolls of Ramsey, Hepmangrove and Bury, 1268–1600* (Toronto, 1990); and Robert B. Goheen, "Peasant Politics? Village Communities and the Crown in Fifteenth-Century England," *American Historical Review* 96 (1991).

Regional and Local Studies

Studies of rural regions and individual villages in medieval England are many, but the following offer good examples of the varieties of perspectives and research methodologies employed by historians today: Anne Reiber DeWindt, "Redefining the Peasant Community in Medieval England: The Regional Perspective," *Journal of British Studies* 26, no. 2

Suggested Readings

(April 1987); Christopher Dyer, *Lords and Peasants in a Changing Society: The Estates of the Bishopric of Worcester, 680–1540* (Cambridge, 1989); Hilda Grieve, *The Sleepers and the Shadows: Chelmsford, a Town, its People and its Past.* Vol. 1: *The Medieval and Tudor Story* (Chelmesford, 1988); Rodney H. Hilton, *A Medieval Society: The West Midlands and the End of the Thirteenth Century* (London, 1966); Marjorie Keniston McIntosh, *Autonomy and Community: The Royal Manor of Havering, 1200–1500* (Cambridge, 1986) and *A Community Transformed: The Manor and Liberty of Havering, 1500–1620* (Cambridge, 1991); Laurence R. Poos, *A Rural Society after the Black Death: Essex, 1350–1525* (Cambridge, 1991); J. Ambrose Raftis, *Warboys: Two Hundred Years in the Life of an English Medieval Village* (Toronto, 1974); Zvi Razi, *Life, Marriage and Death in a Medieval Parish: Economy and Demography in Halesowen, 1270–1400* (Cambridge, 1980); and Sherri Olson, *A Chronicle of All that Happened* (Toronto, 1996).